25 AUTHENTIC BLUES GUITAR LESSONS

by Dave Rubin

T0039561

To access audio visit:
www.halleonard.com/mylibrary

Enter Code
7429-5517-4617-6086

ISBN 978-1-5400-1365-1

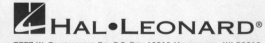

7777 W. BLUEMOUND RD. P.O. BOX 13819 MILWAUKEE, WI 53213

In Australia Contact:
Hal Leonard Australia Pty. Ltd.
4 Lentara Court
Cheltenham, Victoria, 3192 Australia
Email: ausadmin@halleonard.com.au

Visit Hal Leonard Online at
www.halleonard.com

ABOUT THE AUTHOR

Dave Rubin is a New York City blues guitarist, teacher, author, and journalist. He has played with Son Seals, Honeyboy Edwards, Steady Rollin' Bob Margolin, Billy Boy Arnold, Johnny Copeland, Chuck Berry, James Brown's JBs, the Drifters, Marvelettes, Coasters, and the Campbell Brothers. In addition, he has performed on the *Blues Alley* TV show in Philadelphia and *New York Now* in the city and has made commercials for Mountain Dew and the Oreck company.

Dave has been an author for Hal Leonard for more than 25 years and now has nine books in his *Inside the Blues* series to go along with his numerous Signature Licks, Guitar School, and other assorted titles for a total of over 100 books. He was the musical director for the Star Licks DVD series *Legends of the Blues,* as well as being featured in the *12-Bar Blues* accompanying video for his book that was nominated for a Paul Revere Award in 1999.

As a journalist, Dave has written for *Guitar Player, Guitar World, Guitar School, Guitar One, Guitar Edge, Living Blues, Guitar Shop*, and *Blues Access* magazines, and was the recipient of the 2005 Keeping the Blues Alive award in journalism from the Blues Foundation in Memphis, Tennessee.

CONTENTS

B.B. KING

Soloing styles of a modern blues monarch

When B.B. King said, "the blues is just a feeling," he was literally describing his relationship with the art form after more than 60 years. Way past thinking about scales or even individual notes, he played the sound that best expressed his feelings at any given moment. It is at once a very personal sound and one that taps into the universal consciousness, with the results being that virtually every electric guitarist since the early '50s has felt his influence.

Riley B. King was born in the Mississippi Delta on September 16, 1925. He grew up singing gospel music and got his start on the guitar from a preacher uncle. He was an avid record collector, and his early influences were the 78s of Blind Lemon Jefferson and Charlie Christian, eventually expanding to include T-Bone Walker, Johnny Moore, and Django Reinhardt. In the late '40s he relocated to Memphis, Tennessee, where he scored a gig as a DJ on station WDIA. A hip nickname was needed to go with his newfound celebrity status, and so he became known as the "Beale Street Blues Boy," which was shortened to "Blues Boy" King, and then "B.B." King.

His first breakthrough as a recording artist came in 1952 with "Three O'Clock Blues" and his second in 1969 with the crossover hit "The Thrill Is Gone." Around the same time blues and rock guitarists such as Michael Bloomfield and Eric Clapton began singing his praises (after having copped his licks for years!) and, armed with "Lucille" (his Gibson ES-355), he enjoyed bookings at the Fillmore auditoriums and other popular venues. His career maintained a steady profile, with numerous honors as he continued to record and tour with vigor and dignity, until his death in 2015.

For those guitarists who have not quite reached the stage where their blues are a subconscious extension of their creativity, it may be useful to look at some of the elements of B.B.'s style. Though he played all positions of the composite blues scale, he favored the root position **(Fig. 1)** and the one that has euphemistically come to be known as the "B.B. King box" **(Fig. 2)**.

Fig. 3 contains a classic opening lick in the key of G involving the 6th (E) with the 2nd/9th (A) bent a full step to the major 3rd (B) and resolving to the root (G) with "hummingbird" vibrato applied with the index finger.

Fig. 4 shows another opening gambit played out through measures 1–4 of a 12-bar blues. Dig the "signpost" within each chord change that helps to define the tonality: the ♭7th (F) in measure 1, the blues-approved D/B♭ dyad (9th and ♭7th, respectively) in measure 2, the major 3rd (B) in measure 3, and the root (G) in measure 4.

Fig. 5 provides a tantalizing taste of the possibilities available in the "B.B. box." The two primary notes at this position are the root (G) and the 6th (E), which combine for a sweet, consonant sound. Wave after wave of tension provided by the 9th (A) and ♭3rd (B♭) with release to the root keeps the pot boiling.

B.B. King recorded dozens of superlative albums over the years, but if you had to pick just one, make it *Live at the Regal*. With a tone as rich and thick as molasses, "Lucille" soars and B.B. sings rapturously before a deliriously appreciative audience.

Fig. 1

G Composite Blues Scale

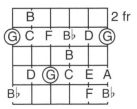

Fig. 2

"B. B. King Box" (Key of G)

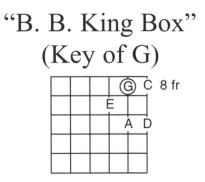

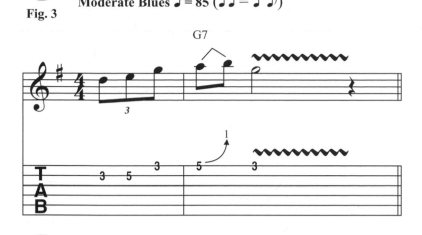

Fig. 3 **Moderate Blues** ♩ = 85

Fig. 4

Moderate Blues ♩ = 90

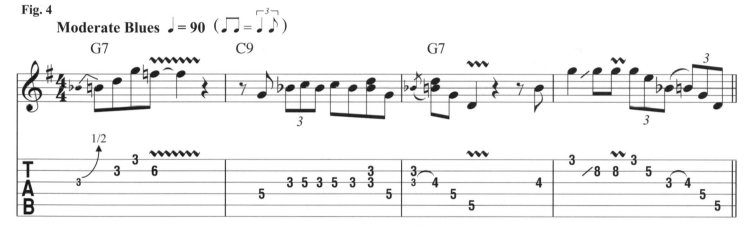

Fig. 5 **Slow Blues** ♩ = 60

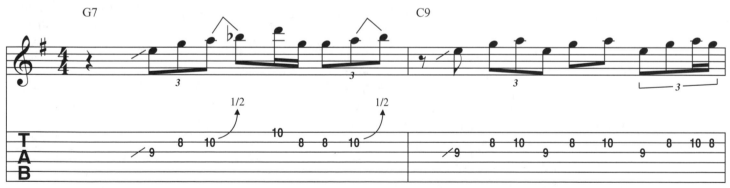

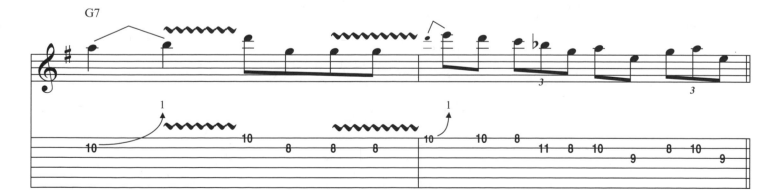

BACK AT THE CHICKEN SHACK

A classic, B-3-inspired, 12-bar jazz-blues

One of the most luscious sounds in postwar music was and still is the combination of a big, fat archtop guitar and a mighty Hammond B-3 organ. The vibrant, tube amp–powered electronic keyboard is capable of creating a massive wall of sound that is infinitely sustainable. When applied to accompanying rhythm parts known as "organ pads," it is the perfect foundation upon which to build a solo. Due to its dynamic, equally warm and resonant qualities, a carved archtop guitar like the Gibson L-5 or Epiphone Emperor blends with and complements the organ like no other instrument. Sonic heaven would not be too strong a description for this celestial sound.

The portable Hammond organ has been around since 1935, and various pioneers literally tried their hands (and feet—the Hammond has a row of bass pedals attached) at making it a new, swinging jazz voice. Starting around 1949, these trail-blazers included "Wild Bill" Davis, who, after leaving Louis Jordan, formed the first organ combo with guitar and drums; Milt Bruckner from the Lionel Hampton band; and Bill Doggett of "Honky Tonk" fame. It would take Philadelphian Jimmy Smith, a true visionary and virtuoso, however, to present to an astonished world the full potential of the Hammond console. The "Jimi Hendrix of the organ," Smith made his debut in the summer of 1955 in Atlantic City, New Jersey, and signed a contract with Blue Note Records in 1956.

The comparison with Hendrix is no idle boast. Smith elicited rave comments like "overwhelming," "futuristic," and "stratospheric" as he rumbled up and down the double keyboards while dancing furiously on the bass pedals. With all shades of the blues at the core of his repertoire, Smith enlisted top session cats like guitarists Eddie McFadden, Quentin Warren, Thornel Schwartz, and particularly Kenny Burrell, to share the spotlight. Usually, it was just a trio with the addition of a drummer, but occasionally, Smith augmented his powerhouse sound with saxophonists Lou Donaldson or Stanley Turrentine.

In 1961, Smith recorded *Back at the Chicken Shack* with Burrell and Turrentine in tow. The title track is a steady grooving 12-bar shuffle with a head that proudly proclaims its blues heritage. Burrell comps under Smith's and Turrentine's initial melodic statement, but these patterns were made for guitarists. The I and IV changes skillfully interweave notes from the G and C Mixolydian mode and blues scale, respectively, to form a composite scale for each chord. I have taken liberties with the phrasing of the original in measures 1, 3, 5, 7, 8, and 11 in order to add swinging eighths on the root notes to fill out the accompaniment. Play these with your thumb, if you can, as it will leave your hand in an advantageous position for accessing the other licks.

A renewed interest in the organ combos of the '60s and '70s occurred in the '90s. Dubbed "acid jazz" (don't ask!), it features classy guitarists like Grant Green, George Benson (pre-Breezin'), Pat Martino, and Burrell, among others, in the company of organists Jack McDuff, Richard "Groove" Holmes, Charles Earland, and Smith. At its best, this music is a perfect marriage between jazz and blues, along with R & B and funk. Playing it will increase your chops and sense of melody while providing musical nourishment for your soul.

BATTLE OF THE BOXES

B.B. King vs. Albert King — two classic blues patterns weigh in

Back in the '50s and '60s, B.B. King and Albert King established themselves as titans of the blues. Albert won over audiences with his crushing bends and caressing touch, while B.B., by contrast, became known for his sensuous vibrato and shimmering, single-note solos. Like their forefather T-Bone Walker, both guitarists worked extensively from the root position of the minor pentatonic scale **(Fig. 1)** early in their careers, but by the mid '60s, Albert had gravitated to a portion of the scale further up the neck **(Fig. 2)** while B.B. leapfrogged even higher yet **(Fig. 3)**. In time, these two scale patterns came to be known as the "Albert King box" and the "B.B. King box," respectively. Each box has its own particular characteristics—especially when it comes to choice string bends—but in reality, both are indispensable to the improvising blues guitarist. Nevertheless, let's see how they stack up against one another.

The Albert King box was actually used by B.B. and others before the '60s, but King Albert turned its manipulation into an art form when he joined the roster at Stax Records in Memphis in 1966. The pattern itself is extremely compact, yet it contains all five notes—root, ♭3rd, 4th, 5th, and ♭7th—of the minor pentatonic scale. For this reason, the box works well over either the I chord or the IV chord.

Fig. 4 shows one of the classic bend licks in this box. **Fig. 5** offers a variation, this time with the addition of the hip bend to the "blue note" in between the ♭3rd (C) and 3rd (C♯) to really ratchet up the tension before the anticipated resolution. Actually, any type of bend on the 1st string that creates tension will resolve easily to the root note (A) at the 10th fret of the 2nd string. **Fig. 6** illustrates a similar concept, as the E (5th) starts out rather neutral but is then followed by the tangy ♭3rd (C) for tension before resolving to

the root (A) over the I chord. Eric Clapton played a lick like this in his tribute to Albert King, "Strange Brew," with the band Cream in 1967.

B.B. King presents a worthy challenge with his box by virtue of a secret weapon: He adds the 9th (B) and the 6th (F♯) to the scale (see Fig. 3). The latter note also functions as the 3rd of the IV (D) chord, making the box especially useful over that chord change. **Fig. 7** demonstrates a dramatic lick that is quite powerful over the I or IV chord. Slide into the F♯ note with your middle finger, plant your index finger on the root (A) note, and bend the B up a full step to the major 3rd (C♯) with your ring finger. While holding the bend, blend the E note with it at the 12th fret with your pinkie. At this point, release the bend and resolve back to the root, adding vibrato.

Fig. 8 contains another dramatic and snappy B.B. lick involving a sweet bend of the E (5th) up to the 6th (F♯). Again, anchor your index finger on the root note, bending the E with your ring finger. Likewise, this lick works great over the I or IV chord. In fact, one of the virtues of this box, as well as Albert's, is that the combination of notes that falls easily under the fingers harmonizes so well with the I and IV chord changes. **Fig. 9** is so slick that it could be repeated over an entire 12-bar chorus, including the V (E) chord.

So who comes out on top? If the history of electric blues is any indication, it is a draw—with guitarists everywhere being the unqualified winners. With immortal string-chokers like Otis Rush, Buddy Guy, Clapton, and Stevie Ray Vaughan, as well as young-bloods such as Jonny Lang, incorporating these boxes into their styles, it is only prudent that you do the same.

Fig. 1 A Minor Pentatonic (Root Position)

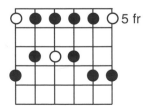

Fig. 2 A Minor Pentatonic (2nd Position)

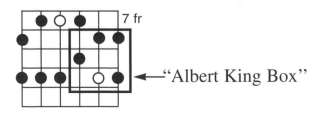

←"Albert King Box"

Fig. 3 A Minor Pentatonic (3rd Position)

■ = added 6th

◉ = added 9th

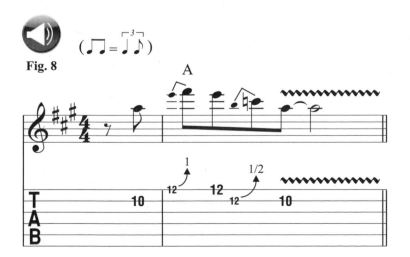

← "B.B. King Box"

Fig. 4

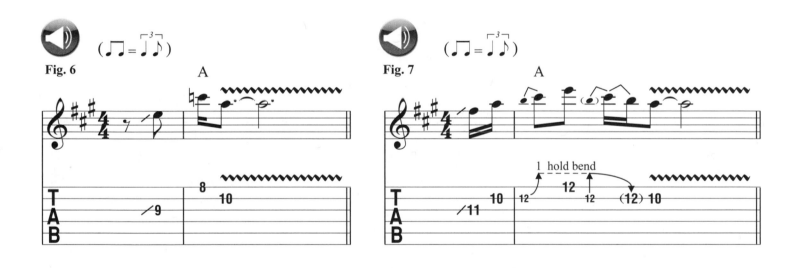

Fig. 5

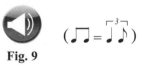

Fig. 6

Fig. 7

Fig. 8

Fig. 9

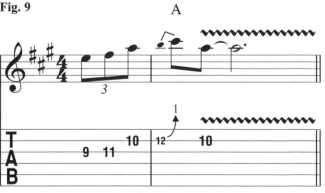

BLUES CHORD SUBSTITUTION

Alternatives for the fundamental I–IV–V progression

The endless fascination with the blues is based on several factors, not the least of which is the bottomless depth of emotion that can be elicited from the musical form. Pre-1900 blues, growing out of work songs and field hollers, was often modal or founded on a one-chord riff like "Catfish Blues." When I–IV–V progressions became the norm in eight- and 12-bar song forms in the 1920s, however, blues music started acquiring different shades of hue, most notably a jazz tinge. This was achieved by inserting various chord voicings and substitutions in place of the standard I–IV–V triads or dominant chords and was practiced by piano players accompanying classic female blues singers like Bessie Smith. Often hailed as the greatest blues singer of all time, she enjoyed the services of Clarence Williams and Fletcher Henderson, among others, in her earliest recordings. Trained in the Dixieland and ragtime genres, they used their harmonic knowledge to extend and embellish beyond what country blues guitarists were playing at the time. It would take until the 1940s, however, before T-Bone Walker, Johnny Moore with Charles Brown, and his brother Oscar with Nat "King" Cole would begin to explore beyond the established perimeters of blues guitar harmony.

Fig. 1 shows measures 1–4 of a 12-bar blues played with common dominant 7th barre chord forms. While this is adequate enough, **Fig. 2** presents a tantalizing taste of just how hip these changes can be with some added spice (i.e. different voicings, chord additions). The A7 and D9 voicings are the most versatile and should be the backbone of your I–IV chord forms. The A13 and D#°7 following the A7 and D9, respectively, provide a sense of anticipation for the next chord change. The IV (D) chord followed by a diminished 7th almost always resolves back to the I chord as indicated. Notice how the top note of each A dominant variation in measures 3 and 4 creates an ascending line based in the A Mixolydian mode, adding a touch of chord melody.

Measures 7 and 8 of a typical 12-bar blues contain the I chord (A). This section is a fertile area of the progression for harmonic invention. **Fig. 3** shows substitute changes for the drab I chord plus some ideas for measures 9 and 10. The figure moves from the I (A) to the VI (F# or G♭—a substitute for the I chord) via chromatic movement that includes the VII (G# or A♭) and ♭VII (G) chords. The V chord could appear next in measure 9 (its usual location), but the II (B) chord followed by the V (E) chord in measure 10 and the standard 1 chord in measure 11 would be more satisfying and set up momentum with a VI–II–V–I cycle of 4ths.

Jazz cats slumming in the blues love the substitute chords in Fig. 4 for measures 7 and 8 of a 12-bar blues. Dig that the point of resolution is still the VI (F#) chord while the ii (Bm7) chord and iii (C#m7) chord substitute diatonically for the I (A). As in Fig. 3, if the II, V, and I chords followed, you would have a cycle of 4ths (C#–F#–B–E–A).

T-Bone Walker took the concept of **Fig. 4** and added another element of substitution as found in **Fig. 5**. It most famously appears in Bobby "Blue" Bland's 1961 version of 'Bone's "Stormy Monday." Instead of the iii (C#m7) chord moving a 4th to the VI (F#9) chord, it descends chromatically to the ♭iii (Cm7) chord, which is a form of tritone substitution. Again, the best chord to follow the Cm7 in measure 9 would be the ii (Bm7) chord, adding to the chromatic movement as well.

Chord substitution is a vast topic worthy of further exploration. These examples are extremely useful in the blues, however, and should be easy to incorporate into your playing after becoming familiar to your ears and hands.

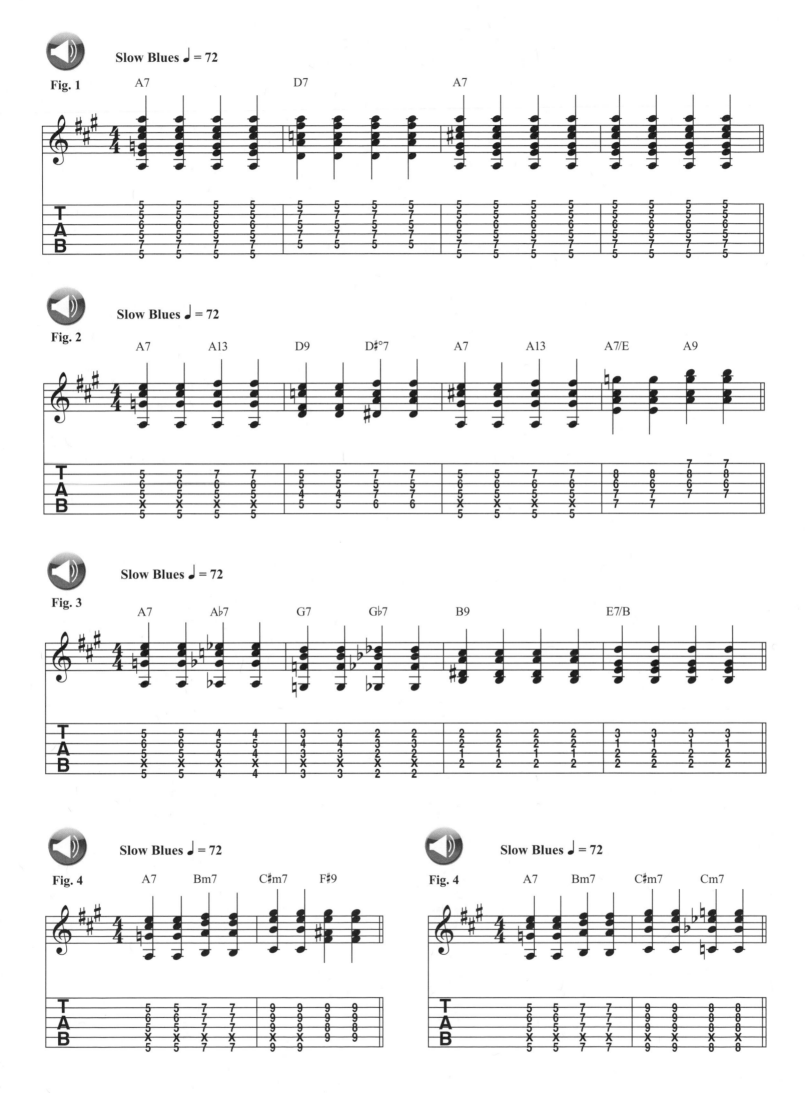

BLUES DELUXE

Riffs, licks, and turnarounds to take your playing to another level

The beauty of blues guitar is that it can be approached in many equally valid ways. Basically, however, there are two main paths to expressive musical fulfillment. The first is the historically accepted "less is more" method, the mode of operation for most blues guitarists until the '60s. The second involves the pursuit of technique and harmonic knowledge for advanced improvisation—which is where we will focus.

Starting with people like Lonnie Mack, Mike Bloomfield, and Eric Clapton, this approach reached its zenith with Stevie Ray Vaughan. Preceding and profoundly influencing this illustrious group were Freddie King, Buddy Guy, and the obscure fret benders Pat Hare and Lafayette "Thing" Thomas.

Of course, you always want to be able to play whatever is appropriate, in blues or any other style. Sometimes one note says it all. But if your playing has become a little stale and you want to expand your vocabulary, then read on. The following "real deal" examples should pump up your chops as well as your chances to claim bragging rights at the next blues jam.

Hot Licks, Chicago Style

The key of E in the open position is the epitome of country blues and, by extension, Chicago blues. Codified by Muddy Waters and Howlin' Wolf and their stellar sidemen Jimmy Rogers and Hubert Sumlin, Chicago blues has a pedigree reaching back to the Mississippi delta and Charley Patton, Son House, and Robert Johnson. **Fig. 1** takes a time-honored phrase and includes a double-string bend to add a dollop of spice. Performance tip: Depending on your string gauge and hand strength, you may want to execute the bends by pulling down with your ring finger. If this is not efficient, try pushing up with your middle finger on string 3 and your ring finger on string 2.

Bending the 4th (A) and 6th (C#) up one-half step creates cool, bluesy harmony with the ♭5th and ♭7th (D). The open G (♭3rd) extends the tension until it is resolved to the root (E), complemented by the slick hammer-on from the ♭3rd to the major 3rd (G#) on beat 1 of measure 2. Be sure to observe the subtle difference between picking the released A and C# notes in measure 1, as opposed to letting the strings sustain in measure 2 from the previous pick stroke.

Fig. 1
♩. = 80
E7

Fig. 2 busts another cliché by showing how to move from box 2 to box 1 (root position) of the blues scale as the chords change from I (A7) to IV (D7). The act of bending and releasing the pitch of B (5th) begins the cycle of tension and resolution in measure 1. Brief resolution to the root (A) is accomplished on beat 2 but is quickly contrasted with the half-step bend to the ♭5th (E♭) and the release to the 4th (D). The "blue" ♭3rd (C) on beats 2 and 3 just naturally wants to resolve to the root on beat 3.

Because phrasing is as important, if not more so, as note selection in the blues, be sure to pay attention to those five even 8th notes, played in the space where three normally reside. This type of lick is especially effective in a slow blues, as it gives the impression of the time slowing and elongating for dramatic effect.

As the chord changes to the IV, the root (D) is nailed with a full-step bend from the ♭7th (C). A series of snappy 16th notes ends the measure by running down the A minor pentatonic scale.

(continued)

Fig. 2

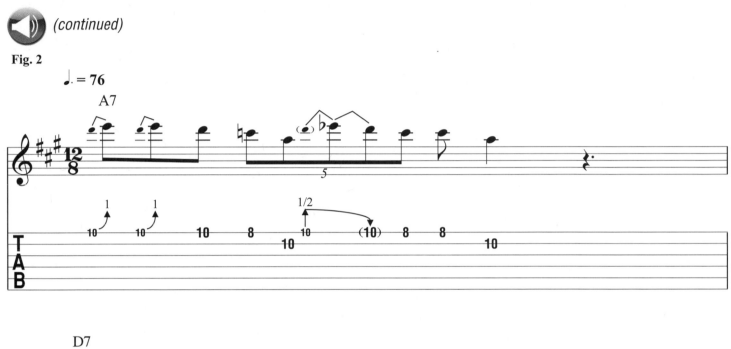

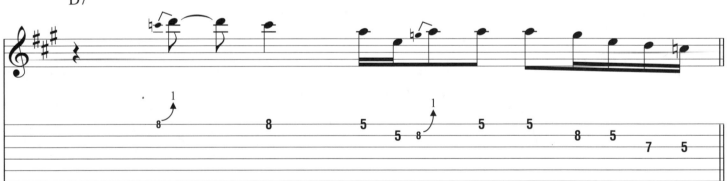

Texas Style

Shuffles did not originate in Texas, although it sometimes seems that way. Perhaps it is the pervasive influence of the swinging "territory bands" that swept through the Southwest in the '30s and '40s that gives Lone Star pickers their steady meter and smooth delivery. Certainly a part of their fluidity is derived from the horn players who were the featured soloists back in the day.

Fig. 3 contains a I (C7)–IV (F7) chord change with horn-like chordal forms. By barring the top three strings with the index finger at fret 8, the I chord is indicated with the additions of the 3rd (E) with the middle finger. The straight barre, depending on context,

usually identifies the IV chord, though here it is used for musical tension via the dissonant but bluesy ♭3rd (E♭).

Measure 2 starts with a similar bend lick, but the half step to the ♭9th (G♭/F♯) provides a touch of jazz harmony. Notice that the C/G notes function as the 5th and 9th of F, where in measure I they functioned as the root and 5th. The notes on beats 2, 3 and 4 (B♭, C, G, and F) from the C blues scale function as the 4th, 5th, 9th, and root of F, respectively. Dig the piggyback bend of B♭ to B(♭5th) to C on beat 2. Be accurate with your intonation and a lick like this will figuratively and literally soar.

(continued)

Fig. 3

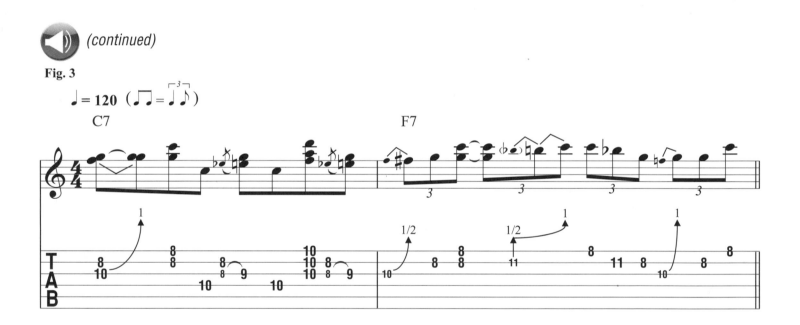

(continued)

Fig. 4

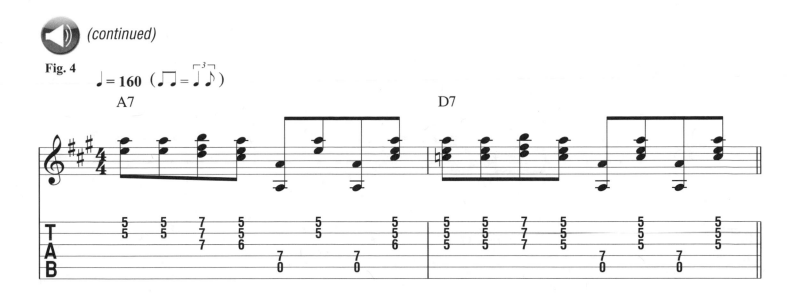

Performing in a guitar-led trio is a fine Texas tradition exemplified by Freddie King and Stevie Ray Vaughan. **Fig. 4** displays triple and double stops combined with bass string octaves for a full, driving sound suggesting two instruments. Again, notice that the I (A) chord is indicated by A/E/C♯ on the "and" of beat 2 in measure 1, while the IV (D7) chord is implied by A/E/C in measure 2.

The B/F♯/D triple stop on beat 2 of measures 1 and 2 implies a jazzy iim (Bm) and I6 (D6), respectively. The alternation of this form works as a great rhythmic and harmonic dynamic when employed in the fashion presented. Performance tip: After striking the octave A notes, allow the open A string to rumble under the other forms to add bottom and cohesiveness.

Blues-Rock Style

Though the line between blues and blues rock has blurred since Lonnie Mack and Mike Bloomfield blasted electric licks into the stratosphere in the early '60s, blues rock still exhibits certain characteristics of traditional blues. Prominent among these are flashy repetitive riffs that engender exciting musical tension. **Fig. 5** shows a series of uncommon triplets in the middle register of the guitar.

The pattern begins with a series of four repeated notes (D-B-B♭-A) fitted into a triplet rhythm, creating a topsy-turvy rhythmic tension. It manages to get back on its feet in the second measure by returning to a more conventional phrasing. Note, however, that the root is used only once (beat 4, measure 2), adding to the dizzy spin of this cool lick. Performance tips: Start with an upstroke and alternate down and up strokes throughout the two measures. Also, keep the parallel As and Ds at the 7th fret clear by rocking your index finger back and forth rather than barring.

Fig. 5

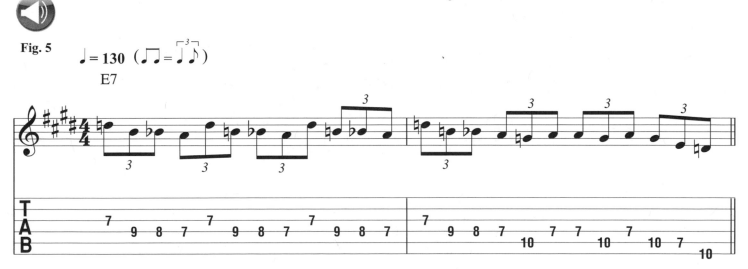

(continued)

Fig. 6 mixes repeating licks and bends in the root position of the E blues scale. A small handful of notes are used but attacked every which way to add interest. The phrase that begins on beat 3 of measure 1 is a classic, but is given an extra dimension by inserting the fretted 5th (B) on beat 4 before the bend. This flows right into another staple of electric blues guitar in measure 2. Favored by sax-influenced players like T-Bone Walker and Chuck Berry, the lick turns into a challenging triplet pattern by the addition of the G note at fret 15 of string 1. At 130 bpm you have to hustle to get around this knuckle-buster!

Jazz Blues Style

Jazz guitarists who get "down in the alley" with the blues, such as Kenny Burrell, George Benson, and Herb Ellis, like to "run through changes" even when they may not be there, creating an "outside" quality to their lines. **Fig. 7** shows a bebop line that seems to run all over the map, but if you envision the changes in parentheses it makes sense. Try this concept with a sparse bass-and-drums accompaniment and see how many goose bumps you raise at your next cutting session. For maximum jazz credibility, avoid the usual "guitaristic" tricks of whole-step bends, hammers and pulls, and instead phrase with a clear pianistic attack.

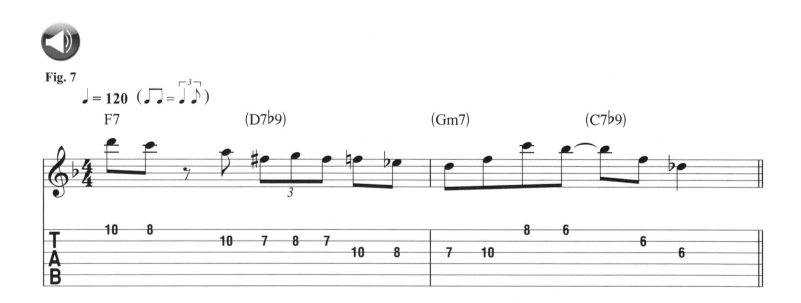

16

Fig. 8 contains measures 1–4 of a sophisticated 16-measure blues progression. The G ionian mode (major scale), with the inclusion of only one blues scale note (B♭), is used exclusively to negotiate the changes. As opposed to the previous example, closer intervals provide a more melodic contour in this phrase. Also, the notes from the G major scale are selected to emphasize the major or dominant qualities of each chord change. For instance, over the G6 chord in measure 1, the root (G), 6th or 13th (E), and major 7th (F♯) notes are played. In measure 3 a whole slew of notes related to C7, including the 3rd (E), 5th (G), and ♭7th (B♭) are presented.

(continued)

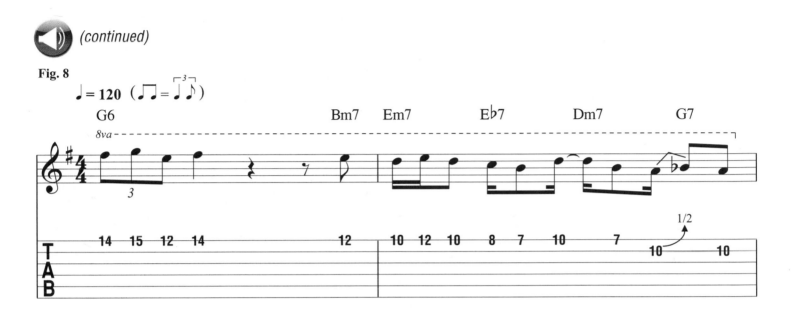

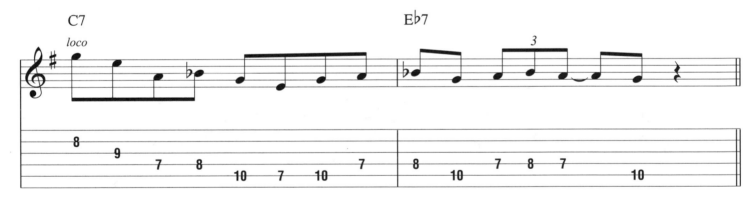

Comping in the groove:
Boogie Patterns

Boogie patterns are the irresistible rhythmic foundation of the blues and a lot of great rock. First recorded on the euphemistic "Lead Pencil Blues" by Johnny Temple in 1935, they were popularized on the immortal tracks cut by Robert Johnson one year later. Though originating in Southern "barrel houses" near the turn of the century by guitarists, piano players would adapt and develop the style to a high degree in the late '30s and early '40s. In the '50s, Elmore James and Jimmy Reed built the major portion of their repertoire on boogie patterns, as did Chuck Berry.

Fig. 9 shows how to embellish a standard, barre chord "cut boogie" pattern. It is called this because it includes only 5ths and 6ths, as opposed to the ♭7th and octaves often favored by piano players. The upper-note stabs on the fourth beat of each measure

imply a quick D-to-A change in the case of measures 1-4, and a D-to-D9 change in measures 5 and 6.

Performance tip: Barre all six strings with your index finger and simply add the major 3rd (C♯) on string 3 with your middle finger after playing the F♯/D double stop with your ring finger. The whole point of this example is to sound like two guitars, so you need to be as quick and smooth as possible when moving from the bass to the treble strings.

Fig. 10 is a reasonable facsimile of piano-style boogie woogie. A bass line "walks" up from the root to the ♭7th and back down to the 3rd. Performance tip: Try playing this fingerstyle by plucking the bass notes with your thumb (or pick) and "block-picking" the chordal forms with your remaining fingers.

Shuffles

The shuffle in **Fig. 11** is sometimes called the "Charleston Rhythm" because the chords are phrased like the classic dance from the Roaring Twenties. The 3rd inversion A9/G appears in Freddie King's "Hide Away" and was also favored by Robert Lockwood, Jr. and Stevie Ray Vaughan. Notice how the "voices" (individual notes within the chord) move smoothly to the D9 chord. This chord is a bit of a stretch in the lower positions, but provides a great big ringing sound.

Most shuffles are in major keys, but a minor-key shuffle has an allure all its own. **Fig. 12** contains a two-measure (repeated), moveable pattern similar to, of all songs, Michael Jackson's "Billie Jean." Performance tip: Strum down with a sharp rhythmic snap.

Slow Blues

Fig.13 shows a way to keep the deep blues feeling while freshening up the harmony. Like **Fig.11**, close voice leading between the G13/F and the C9/E is paramount to this seductive sound. Notice that the root note in the G13 chord is the highest, rather than the lowest, note in the form.

Funk Blues

It is not known if Muddy Waters had an opinion about funk blues, but Texas bluesmaster Albert Collins must have dug the style due to his propensity to play it with gusto throughout his career. **Fig.14** is similar to Jr. Walker & the Allstars' "Shotgun" and Alvin Cash & the Crawlers' "Twine Time." Of course, those songs are one-chord vamps, whereas we blues cats would arrange these riffs into a I-IV-V 12-bar progression. Also, note that the G7#9 chord comes from jazz and is a favorite of funk musicians, as well as Mr. Hendrix.

Fig. 14

Turnarounds

Turnarounds are to blues guitarists what a good slider is to a fastball pitcher: They separate the journeyman from the ace of the staff. Frankly, you can't know too many turnarounds, as they lend distinction to repetitive 12- or 8-bar blues choruses. **Fig.15** contains a fat open-string turnaround in the modern guitarist's key of A. Having the root note appear on the open A string and the wide intervals stacked on top make this turnaround more appropriate for loud, distorted electric guitars than some other open-string turnarounds that sound indistinct at high volume.

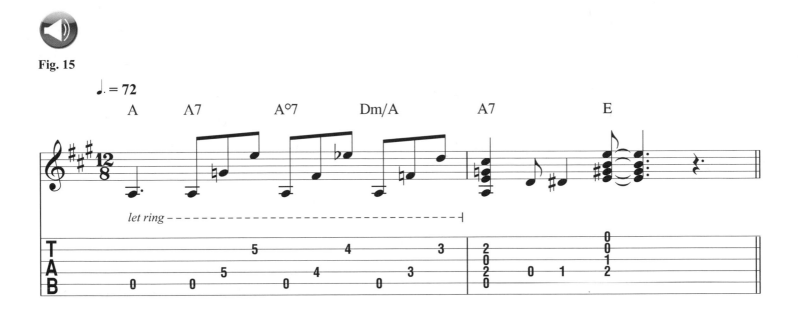

Fig. 15

Fig.16 presents a lush, moveable turnaround capable of filling up a considerable amount of harmonic space. Starting with the "Hide Away" chord (A9/G), first shown in **Fig. 11**, and resolving to the open position triad, it has a classical effect know as "contrary motion," where the notes on string 2 ascend while those on string 4 descend at the same time. As opposed to **Fig. 15**, the root (A) note is on string 1 and provides the tonal center against which the moving harmonies interact.

(continued)

Fig. 16

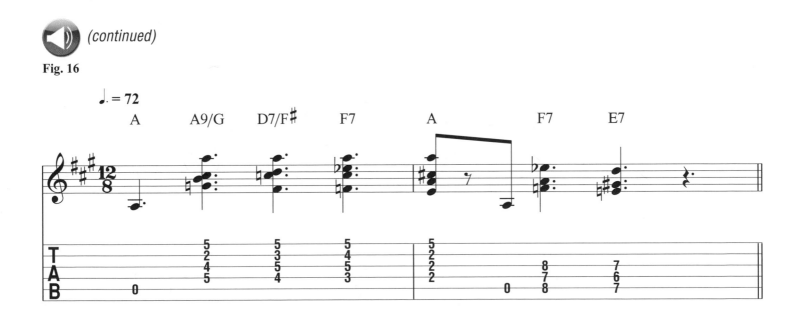

BLUES SCALES & TARGET NOTES

Choosing carefully to make choice solos

Like a witch's strange brew, superior blues solos comprise a blend of ingredients that may seem mystifying. Boiled down to the essentials, they are killer tone, soulful phrasing and tasty, intelligent note selection. The most objective of the three is note selection—specifically note selection based on target notes. This will be the focus of our exploration. The knowledge is neither difficult to understand or apply, and, with it, your playing will acquire greater depth of expression as you add structure to your solos. This information will cut the fat and build real muscle into your chops.

Playing a hot blues solos is comparable to taking a musical journey and telling a good story along the way—the chord progression is your highway and the target notes are your sign posts. The most common blues progressions are 12 bars in length and fall into two patterns. **Fig. 1** shows the most basic, with the fewest actual chord changes. It is often used in mid-tempo shuffle blues like Stevie Ray Vaughan's "Pride and Joy" and Freddie King's "Tore Down," which was covered by Eric Clapton on *From the Cradle*. I have chosen to express the chord changes with the 5th-to-6th comping figure popularized by Robert Johnson ("Sweet Home Chicago," "Dust My Broom") and Chuck Berry ("Johnny B. Goode," "Carol").

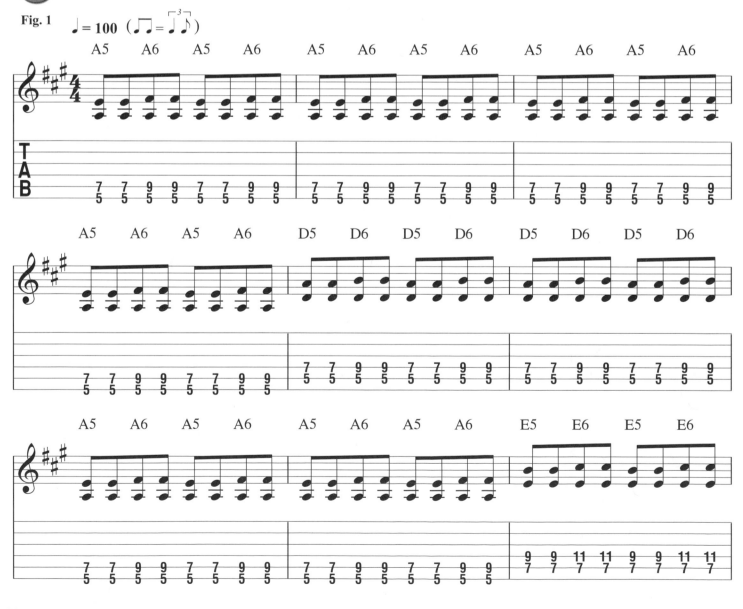

22

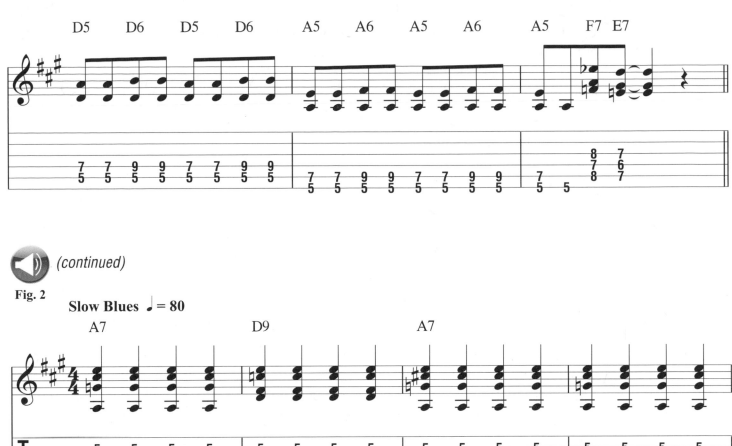

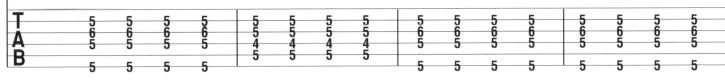

(continued)

Fig. 2

Slow Blues ♩ = 80

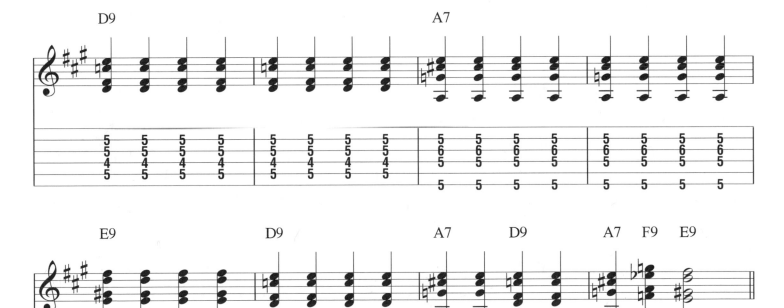

The second pattern **[Fig. 2]**, with its more active chord changes, is the basis for many slow blues including Guitar Slim's "The Things I Used to Do" and Larry Davis' "Texas Flood" (the title tune from Stevie Ray Vaughan's first album). The seventh and ninth chord voicings used in this example are standard yet versatile blues chords. Note that you could reverse this situation and play the 5th-to-6th comping figure for the slow blues, and the seventh and ninth chords for the shuffle. Give it a try. These progressions will be the ground we traverse with our solo improvisations.

Musicians of all stripes use Roman numerals derived from the scale steps of the major scale when referring to chords. So shall we, even though our concern here is with just the three chords that form the backbone of almost all blues. They are the I, IV and V. **Fig. 3** depicts the A major scale (Ionian mode) from which you can derive the chords A, D, and E. (Note: The F9 chord in measure 12 of Figures 1 and 2 is a passing chord to E, the V.)

Fig. 3 A Major Scale

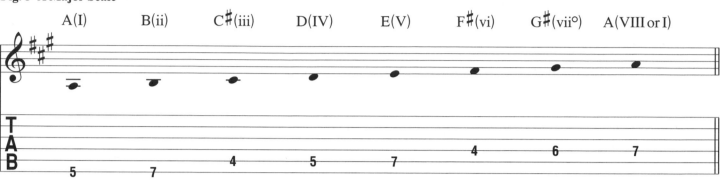

Fig. 4 illustrates the A blues scale. The steps in this six-note scale are A (root), C (minor third), D (fourth), E♭ (diminished fifth), E (fifth) and G (minor seventh). With this scale, we will see how a rudimentary yet effective solo can be constructed over a 12-bar blues.

This brings us to a necessary discussion of *target notes*—the melody notes that help emphasize or outline a particular chord's sound when soloing over a progression. If skillfully applied within a particular lick or phrase, they add melodic substance and definition.

Fig. 5 shows the target notes for the I, IV and V chords within the scope of this blues scale. The goal is to aim for these notes when soloing over a given chord. Do not let the repetition of notes among the three changes confuse you. Remember, the function or destination of the scale tones change with each chord—the C note, for example, sounds and functions differently on the I chord as opposed to the IV chord. (Context is everything when improvising in any style of music.) Also, be aware that the C, as the flat third or minor third, is idiomatic to the blues. It acts as a spicy "blue note" when played against major or dominant-type seventh chords which contain a major third. It is especially "bluesy," in an idiomatic melodic sense, over the I chord when it resolves to the root (A, in this case), as in the ending part of a phrase or lick.

Fig. 4 A Blues Scale

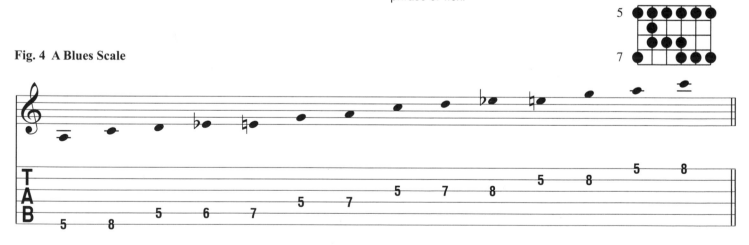

Fig. 5 Target Notes from the A Blues Scale

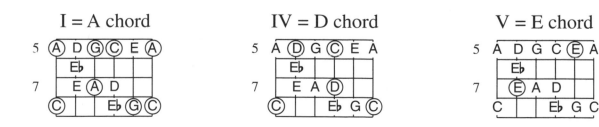

Fig. 6 Moderate Blues/Shuffle

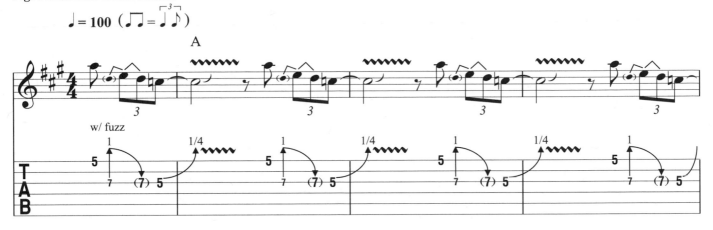

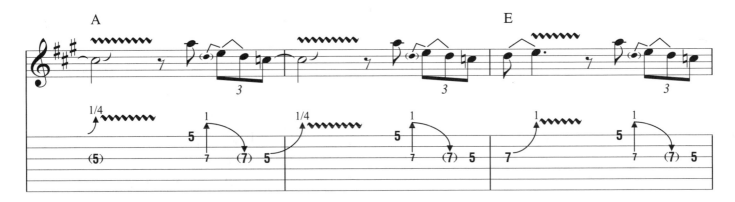

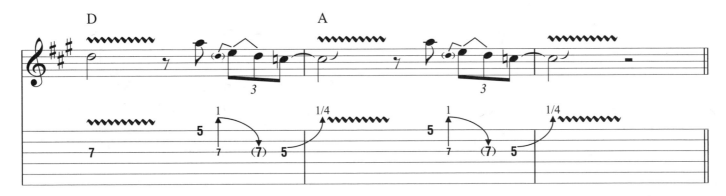

Fig. 6 is reminiscent of Eric Clapton's early style. It's a repeating lick with the last note acting as the target note to nail the chord change. Target notes can occur anywhere in a phrase and they can appear more than once. They are used to best advantage, though, as either the *first* or *last* note. Try playing this solo over the chord progression in **Fig. 1**.

A world of great blues and rock guitar music, from Blind Lemon Jefferson to Guns N' Roses, has been created around the minor pentatonic scale, the most basic of the blues scales. An equally impressive repertoire has sprung from the blending of the jazzy Mixolydian mode with the minor pentatonic scale. **Fig. 7** illustrates the A Mixolydian mode, and **Fig. 8** the "hybrid blues Mixolydian scale" that results from superimposing one over the other. Notice there is only one difference between the Mixolydian mode and the major scale—the flat or minor seventh instead of the major seventh. It is critical, however, because it is the note which differentiates a major chord from a dominant-type seventh chord and its related dissonant family (9th, 11th and 13th chords). Since blues progressions are constructed on dominant-type seventh chords, it stands to reason that the Mixolydian mode in blues soloing reinforces a close relationship.

Notice that the hybrid scale does not contain all the notes from both scales. Instead, I have pared it down to reflect the form used by B.B. King and his legions of followers. The "King of the Blues" was heavily influenced by jazz guitarists Charlie Christian and Django Reinhardt, as well as blues masters T-Bone Walker and Lonnie Johnson. Each of these legendary players was conversant with the Mixolydian mode.

In **Fig. 9**, I have staked out the target notes from this "new and improved" scale. The addition of the major third (C#) for the I chord throws the flat third (C) into a different perspective and corrects a limitation of the basic minor pentatonic scale—the I chord gains a note for its exclusive use. Then, if desired, we can relegate the flat third to the IV chord where it functions well as the flat seventh of the chord.

Fig. 10 is a 12-bar slow blues solo like B.B.'s "Sweet Little Angel" and Davis' "Texas Flood." After you have the licks firmly under your fingers, play them over the changes of **Fig. 2**. Hearing the note-to-chord relationships will greatly facilitate your understanding of the concepts we have been exploring. The strong sense of movement from the I chord to the IV should be particularly striking. This particular chord change has a strong momentum, or forward motion, in blues chord changes, and is at the heart of much blues-based music. The hippest and best way to define the I-IV change melodically is to emphasize the major third (C#) over the I and the flat third (C) over the IV, as noted throughout the example. Be sure to see that the combination of the major third and flat seventh (C# and G) of the I7 chord in measures 3 and 4, and the flat seventh and root (C and D) of the IV9 chord in measures 5 and 10 produces a definitive blues effect. Furthermore, the flat third can act as a passing tone to get you to the major third of the I chord (measures 1, 3 and 11)—a practice that is 100% blues approved!

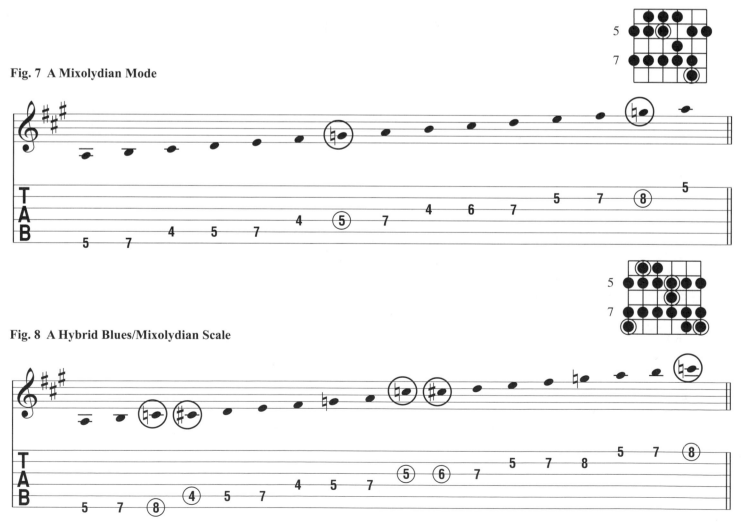

Fig. 7 A Mixolydian Mode

Fig. 8 A Hybrid Blues/Mixolydian Scale

Fig. 9 Target Notes from Hydrib Blues/Mixolydian Scale

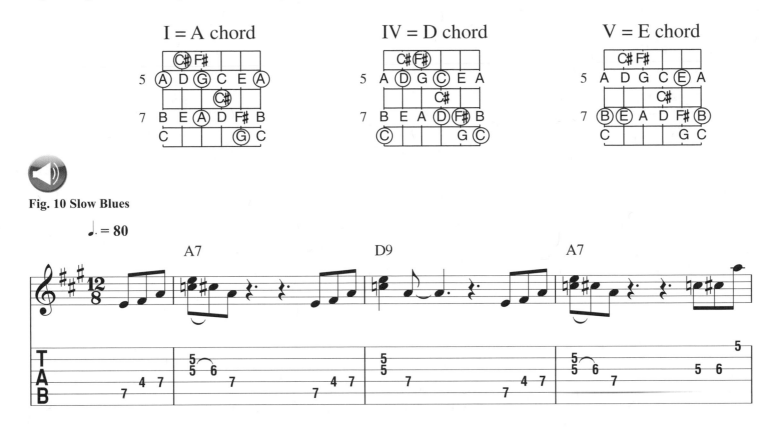

Fig. 10 Slow Blues

♩. = 80

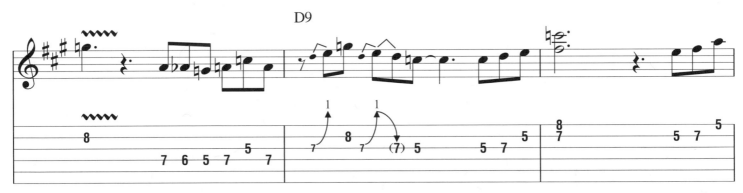

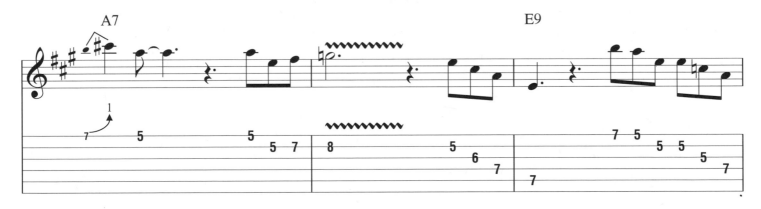

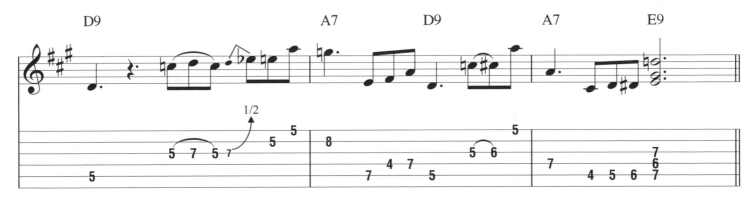

Figs. 11 and 11A show two other classic ways to motor from the I to the IV with flair. They contain a combination of major and minor triads (A/C♯ and Am/C), and diminished triads functioning as three-note dominant-type seventh chords—a common blues device. If you're wondering, that A/C♯ triad does sound like the familiar slide guitar lick from Elmore James' version of "Dust My Broom." Likewise, the pattern of **Fig. 11A** evokes one of Robert Johnson's many contributions to the language of the blues. It can be found in his "32-20," as well as Muddy Waters' "Long Distance Call." Try substituting these triads for the first three bars of **Fig. 10**. The fourth measure (I chord) often has a contrasting phrase of single notes to break away from the pattern and shoot for the next IV chord change. This is what you find in the last measures of **Figs. 11 and 11A**.

Don't despair if the target notes are foreign to your fingering habits. You can easily train your middle finger to fall on the major third as readily as your first finger lands on the flat third. However, the art of blues soloing is beyond the acquisition of motor skills and pure technique—it is about phrasing, conviction and rhythmic placement of melody. Remember, just as Duke Ellington wrote, "It don't mean a thing if it ain't got that swing," and Willie Dixon said "It's not the meat, it's the motion," it is the quality not the quantity of the notes you play that matter!

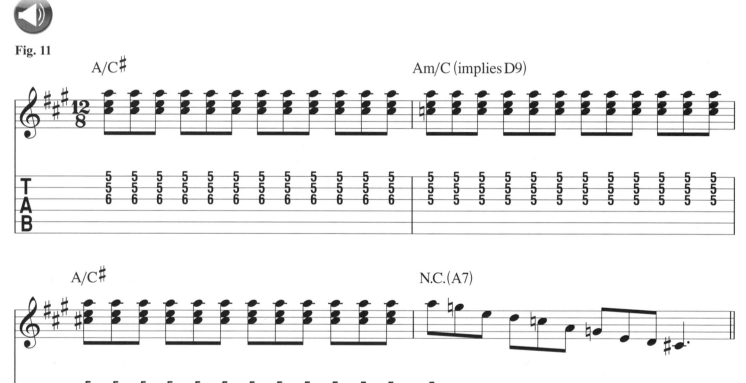

Fig. 11

Fig. 11A

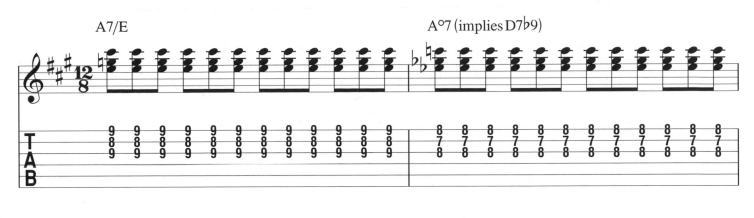

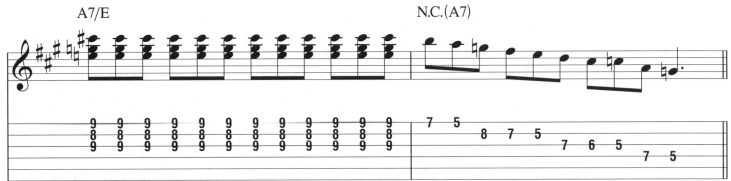

BLUES VAMPS

Build a firm foundation with these rock-solid riffs

The roots of the blues are at once prosaic and profound. Developed in the Deep South decades before the Civil War, they consisted of work songs derived from traditional African sources, and from field hollers. Anne Kimble, the wife of a Georgia rice planter, wrote in her journal in 1838–1839 of hearing the slaves in the fields singing "extraordinarily wild and unaccountable. The way in which the chorus strikes in with the burden between each phrase of the melody chanted by a single voice is very curious and effective."

This "call and response" of the work song would also be repeated in field hollers, where the slaves communicated with each other by singing the information they wished to "pass under the master's nose." When the banjo, harmonica, and guitar made their way onto the plantations after the war, it's likely that the instruments were used to imitate these vocal mannerisms.

Before the blues was codified with I–IV–V chord changes and regular eight-, 12-, and 16-bar verses in the 1920s, mono-chord riffs and licks, also known as "vamps," were the artistic coin of the realm. Though eventually functioning as the formal elements of musical entertainment, they grew out of the unstoppable need for an oppressed populace to maintain and cultivate their unique culture.

Fig. 1 is probably an outgrowth of a specific variety of work song known as an "axe-fall." The downbeat of "one" in each measure (the E chord immediately following the G/D) is where the axe (or sledgehammer on a train track crew) would fall in order to synchronize the laborers at their task. Son House's "Walking Blues" is a famous example of this type of axe-fall rhythm placed in a 12-bar format, while "I'm a Man" by Bo Diddley is the derivation for the figure shown.

The finger-snapping riff in **Fig. 2** has a pedigree that stretches from country blues to swing and R & B. This pattern has a tremendous amount of drive at any tempo and makes for a great intro or coda, as well as the foundation of a hip groove tune. Notice that the phrasing is similar to the horn riff under Bill Evans' piano solo in Miles Davis' "So What."

Fig. 3 is a Chicago blues bass riff that, while constructed from the blues scale and containing the familiar octave (A) and ♭7th (G), is phrased quite differently from most related patterns, as it has an implied syncopation that moves toward R & B and rock. Billy Boy Arnold's "I Wish You Would" is based on a similar vamp and was a landmark recording in the mid '50s.

Both "Green Onions" by Booker T. and the MGs and Sonny Boy Williamson's "Help Me" utilized patterns like **Fig. 4** to produce memorable results. The harmonic sequence of I (A)–♭III(C)–IV(D) is found in several of John Lee Hooker's boogie classics and most prominently displayed in Z.Z. Top's "La Grange." Dig that in essence it's a I–IV vamp, arguably the most influential in popular music.

Fig. 5 is based on "Mannish Boy" by Muddy Waters, the all-time, bone-crushing champ. Like Fig. 1, it gains power via the dramatic musical rest on beats 2 and 3. Can anyone ever forget the scene in *Goodfellas* when Ray Liotta's character gets in his car on the fateful morning and Muddy's voice comes in singing, "Oh yeah," and the band enters with the riff?

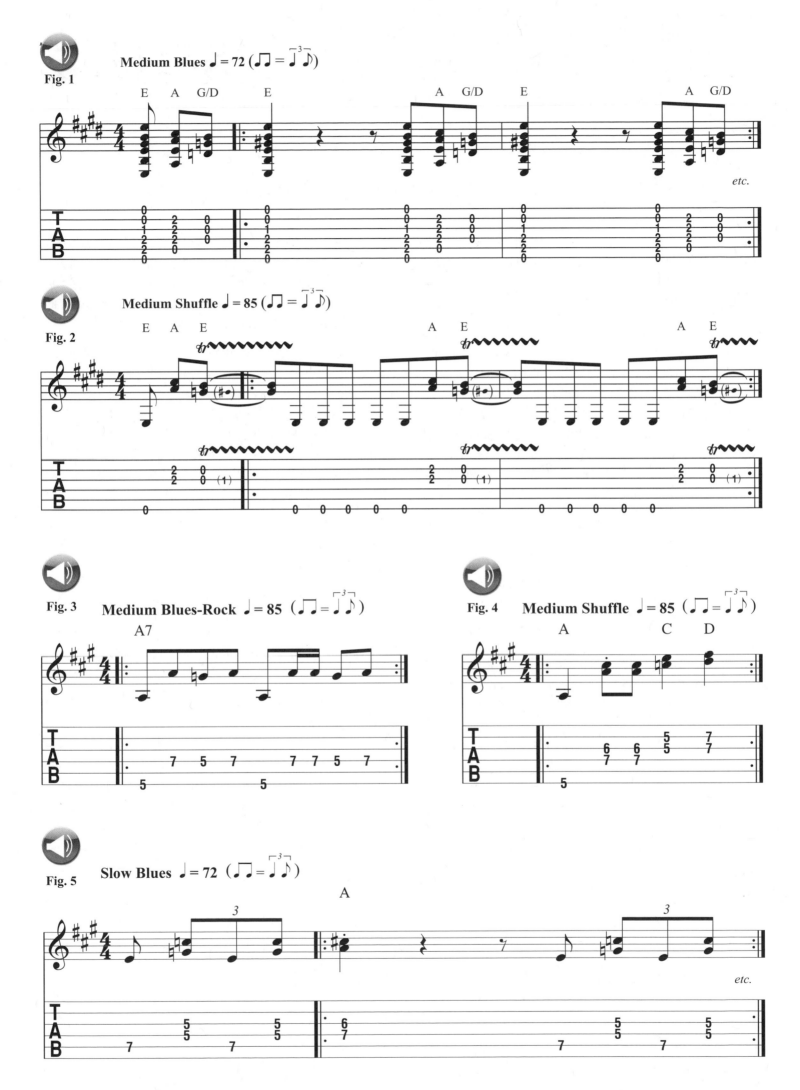

BOOGIE WOOGIE ALTERNATIVES

Five substitutions for standard boogie-based accompaniments

Boogie woogie rhythms have been around for more than 100 years, and have provided the powerful driving wheels for innumerable classic blues. When modified from a swing or shuffle feel into straight 4/4, they have also been the source of inspiration for Chuck Berry, the Rolling Stones, and their countless followers.

Developed in lumber, mining, and turpentine camps in the South just after the Civil War, the roots of boogie woogie music were developed by the interplay of two or three guitarists as they entertained their fellow workers. One guitarist would pick single-string lines while another "seconded" him with "framming," or chordal accompaniment. If a third guitarist was available, he would bang on the lower strings as if playing a tom-tom. Together they created an irresistible dance rhythm that, like a host of blues forms, was derived from the sound of chugging locomotives.

Toward the end of the 19th century, pianos began to appear in the "barrelhouses" that served as juke joints in the camps. As the rowdy patrons still wanted to hear the same exhilarating rhythms formerly performed by the guitarists, piano players transferred and expanded the bass string patterns to their left hands as a steady accompaniment to the bluesy riffs executed in the higher registers by the right hand. Concurrently, country blues guitarists continued experimenting with the form into the early 20th century. Blind Lemon Jefferson, the legendary Texas axeman, was heard to play a moving bass line in 1911 as he sang about a "booger rooger," or house party. By the early '30s, Delta blues guitarist Johnny Temple was playing "cut-boogie" patterns with 5ths and 6ths (omitting the ♭7th) that would have a tremendous influence on Robert Johnson in songs like "Sweet Home Chicago" and "(I Believe) I'll Dust My Broom."

Artistically, boogie woogie would reach its zenith in the late '30s and early '40s in the muscular hands of pianists Pete Johnson, Meade Lux Lewis, and Albert Ammons. It achieved its peak popularity, however, during World War II, when every swing band of note had a crowd-pleasing boogie-woogie arrangement.

As appealing and versatile as those forms are, it is prudent to know a wide variety of alternative, boogie-based accompaniments. These figures will all be in the key of A, but be sure to move them around to other keys once you get the hang of them. **Fig. 1** shows a bass line that "walks" through the root, ♭3rd, and 4th notes of the blues scale relative to the I (A), IV (D), and V (E) chords. Booker T. & the MGs' "Green Onions" and Sonny Boy Williamson's "Help Me" both use this line as their foundation and as a rhythmic hook.

Fig. 2 contains the same concept harmonized with chords and presents a big, powerful accompaniment. Be aware that ZZ Top's "Tush" is a variation on this theme.

Fig. 3 has appeared as the underpinning in numerous blues tunes, including Freddie King's instrumental "Heads Up" and, altered, in Little Richard's "Lucille." In **Fig. 4** the 5th, ♭7th, and octave notes have been harmonized with double stops to create a more sophisticated tonality via the combination of the interval of a minor 3rd (beat 2) and the 4ths that follow (beats 3 and 4).

Fig. 5 is a bass line constructed from the 1st, 2nd, and 3rd scale degrees of the major scale. The harmonization (string 4) is built on the interval of a 6th and uses the ♭7th of the Mixolydian mode. This gives it a more melodic contour than the previous examples, and it is quite "pianistic" in flavor. Playing the notes on string 6 with the pick while simultaneously plucking the notes on string 4 with the middle finger will help contribute to this aural illusion.

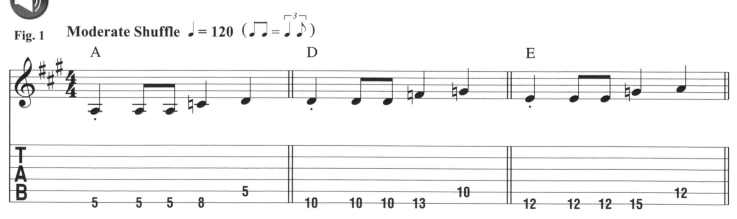

Fig. 1 Moderate Shuffle ♩ = 120

BOTTLENECK BLUES

A crash course on standard-tuned slide

Many organic sounds have been copped on synthesizers over the years, including those of electric guitars. Jan Hammer, the keyboard wizard who played with John McLaughlin and Jeff Beck, once did a version of Hendrix's "Manic Depression" that was pretty scary in its mimicry of a wildly distorted guitar. But rest assured, no pitch wheel on a synth will ever duplicate the subtle microtones, expressive vibrato, and tactile sense of dynamics that can be produced by slide guitar.

Music historians still debate whether blues guitarists around 1900 thought of laying bone, bottle, or jack knife against the strings of their guitars on their own, or were influenced by Hawaiian guitarists. One of the earliest descriptions of the technique, however, was by W.C. Handy, the "Father of the Blues," who recalled hearing a slide guitarist for the first time in Mississippi in 1903.

Most country-blues guitarists played slide in open tunings like G, A, E, and D. Honey Boy Edwards has always been one of the few exceptions to play in standard tuning. Other great players who mastered this approach were Tampa Red, Robert Nighthawk, Earl Hooker, and Muddy Waters, in his later years. It is more difficult to play cleanly and harmoniously in standard tuning due to the preponderance of 4ths—as opposed to the more chordal 3rds and 5ths afforded in open tunings. However, it is much easier to visualize the fingerboard in standard tuning, making one less major issue to deal with while gaining control of accurate intonation and damping.

Slides come in different materials, the most popular being brass, chromed steel, and glass. The old-timers made their own from the neck of a spirits bottle, hence the name "bottleneck." Brass gives a dark, fat sound with lots of overtones and sustain (good for acoustic guitars with heavy strings, and hollowbody electrics); steel, a somewhat lighter, harder sound with sustain; and glass, a smooth, bright, transparent tone with less sustain (good for electric solidbody guitars, especially Strats). Basically, the heavier the slide—regardless of material—the better the sustain. It is recommended that the slide be worn on the pinky, to allow the other three fingers the freedom to fret other notes. Whatever slide you choose, make sure that it fits snugly and is long enough to span the width of the fingerboard.

Damping of unwanted vibrations and accurate intonation are paramount to acceptable slide guitar technique. You must lightly drag your free fingers behind the slide on the strings to mute the ones you are not picking. Also, you should keep the heel of your picking hand close to the bridge so that you can drop it on top of the bridge when you wish to effectively dampen all string vibration. In terms of intonation, remember that the correct pitch is sounded when the slide is directly over the fret wire. You will want to press down hard enough to make solid contact with the string, but not so hard that you touch the string to the fret. High action and heavier strings will go a long way toward a clean sound. Serious slide guitarists often keep an axe just for slide, and jack up the action using .011, .012, or heavier gauge strings.

One of the secrets to great slide playing is to follow each chord change, especially for blues. **Fig. 1** shows three slide positions that correspond to the I, IV, and V chords in the key of C. Record a slow blues in the key of C to play over, and practice moving to the appropriate fret position as the chords change. Try arpeggiating the three notes at frets 5, 10, and 12, and use the two notes on strings 1 and 2 to connect your position shifts. Once you're comfortable with attaining good intonation, try adding some vibrato to your notes—this is the most expressive aspect of slide guitar playing.

Fig. 1 I, IV, and V Chords in the Key of C

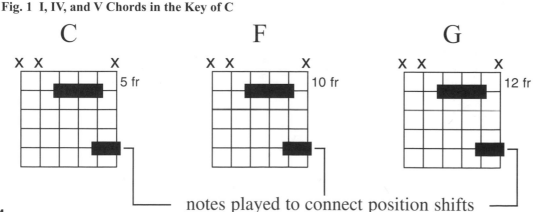

notes played to connect position shifts

Fig. 2 is based on the classic slide lick from Elmore James' version of "Dust My Broom." Elmo' played his in open D, a nasty, brutish tuning that we will touch on in a future column. We can sound just as "bad" in standard tuning, however, by cranking the distortion on our amps to maximum overdrive. By the way, those triplets in measure 1 will sound bluesier if you slide into them from roughly one fret below on each beat.

Fig. 3 is an introduction in the style of Muddy Waters. Dig that the pattern in measure 2 comes from the C minor pentatonic scale. This is acceptable in standard tuning as long as you end your phrase on a strong chordal tone (root, 5th, or ♭7th will do nicely). Let's try to

avoid the ♭3rd over a major or dominant chord. Be aware that the turnaround in measure 3 will sound cleaner if you simultaneously attack the notes on string 4 with your pick and pluck the notes on string 2 with your middle finger.

Slide is one of the most demanding but rewarding techniques to be addressed on the guitar. Go slowly, and strive for accurate intonation and a clean sound above all else. Unlike straight fretting, this way of playing does not require a lot of notes to be effective. On the contrary, a handful of choice notes, vibratoed with conviction, will make for the most memorable musical statement.

Fig. 2 "Elmore James Lick"

Fig. 3 à la Muddy Waters

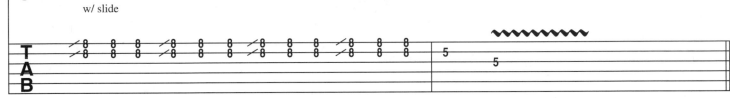

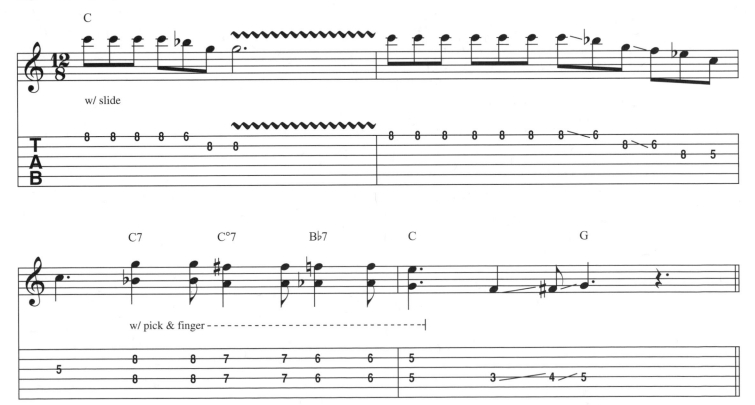

BRITISH BLUES-ROCK

Blues from across the Atlantic

One of the great ironies in the history of postwar blues is that the British, after their rock invasion in the early '60s, proceeded to bring our blues back to us in the mid '60s. Free from the racial and sociological baggage that plagued (and still plagues) the blues in America, the British had welcomed Big Bill Broonzy, Muddy Waters, and the various American Folk Blues Festivals sponsored by the State Department in the late '50s and early '60s. The Rolling Stones, John Mayall and his Bluesbreakers, the Animals, Fleetwood Mac, the Yardbirds, and Led Zeppelin, among others, absorbed American rural and urban blues to a remarkable degree, and then turned them into a new style called blues-rock. Though based on traditional blues forms, it was often played faster, louder, and more distorted than the original sources.

Lonnie Donegan is credited as putting the first "blues" record on the English charts with his "skiffle" version of "Rock Island Line" in 1954. As the decade wore on, interest in "pure" acoustic and folk blues built until the early '60s, when electric Chicago blues was discovered and finally accepted. By then the "Father of British Blues," Alexis Korner, and his Blues Incorporated band had become a virtual graduate school for aspiring blues musicians like Cyril Davies (who claimed Jeff Beck among his All Stars at one point), Graham Bond, John Mayall, and the Stones. Of these, Mayall would prove to be the most influential, helping to launch the careers of Eric Clapton, Peter Green, and Mick Taylor. A fine interpreter in his own right, he continues to perform and record.

The British blues scene has produced a wealth of other great blues-based bands and guitarists over the years, including Rory Gallagher, Tony "T.S." McPhee and the Groundhogs, the Spencer Davis Group (with Stevie Winwood on keyboards and guitar), the Aynsley Dunbar Retaliation, and Gary Moore, formerly of Thin Lizzy. In addition, no survey would be complete without mentioning Alvin Lee of Ten Years After fame. Depending on your point of view, his barrage of well-articulated notes is either the zenith or nadir of the genre.

Fig. 1 is an example of the type of single-note accompaniment line that Eric Clapton might play on an uptempo blues. Though improvised, the fact that it is confined to the bass strings helps to keep it in the rhythm section's sonic space, along with the bass and keyboards, and out of the way of the vocalist. Clapton's use of the C Mixolydian mode provides the melodic major 3rd (E) to help define the C major tonality, along with the root (C), 5th (G), and ♭7th (B♭) notes. Observe the way he bends the ♭7th a quarter step up to the "true blue note" between the ♭7th and the major 7th (B), in addition to goosing it up an extra quarter step to the surprisingly melodic (and diatonic) major 7th.

Jeff Beck, out of all his contemporaries from the '60s, has never stopped growing as an innovative improviser without peer. Even back in his blues days with the Yardbirds and the first Jeff Beck Group, he was pushing the envelope. **Fig. 2** displays how he would begin a phrase with a standard blues idea (the 4th bent to the 5th followed by the root) and develop it into an ear-opening climax (the root bent to the 9th).

British bands often expanded upon classic blues riffs in the '70s. **Fig. 3** is inspired by "I'm a Man" in the manner that a heavy blues-rock group like Foghat might interpret it. See the way it builds from a single-note riff to one with chords, and then a combination of bass notes and lead fills.

Fig. 1

Medium Blues ♩ = 120 (♫ = ♩³♪)

Fig. 2

Medium Shuffle ♩ = 120 (♫ = ♩³♪)

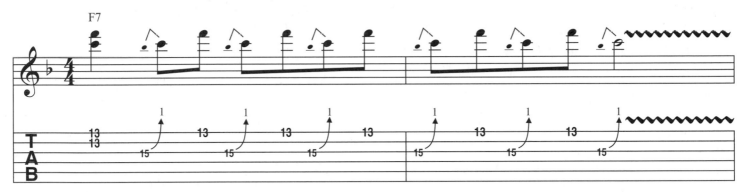

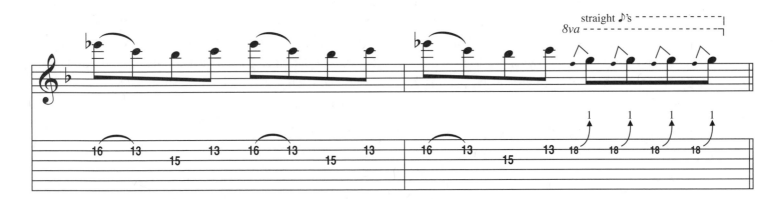

Fast Blues-Rock ♩ = 130

Fig. 3

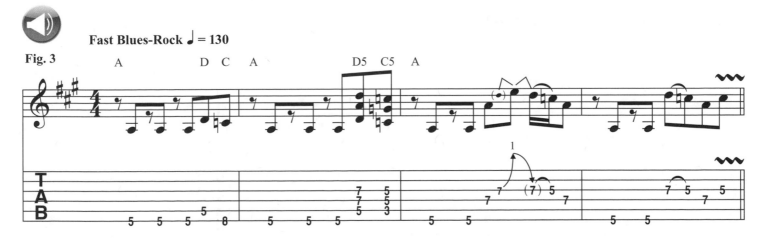

CATFISH BLUES

The evolution of a classic lick

Why a catfish? Bluesmen may have liked it as a metaphor for their own adaptability and survival, as catfish are hardy creatures that have been on the earth a long time. Pan-fried, they are a delicacy available to anyone with a fishing pole, which could help to explain the lyric "I wish I was a catfish, swimming in the deep blue sea. I'd have all these good-lookin' women, fishing after me." Whatever the exact interpretation of the content, the form of "Catfish Blues" is derived from one of those deep Delta guitar licks that goes back to the origins of the music.

The earliest version of "Catfish Blues" was recorded in 1941 by Robert Petway and shows no evidence of the licks that have come to define the song, having instead a syncopated chordal pattern that could literally be a precursor of funk. That same year, however, Tommy McClennan cut "Deep Blue Sea Blues," with the same lyric idea and licks that evolved to become the classic hook. In 1950, Muddy Waters made "Rolling Stone" with the "Catfish" lyrics and a form of the lick in the intro that Hendrix would later refine (and credit to Muddy). Then in 1951, John Lee Hooker, Bobo "Slim" Thomas, and Muddy Waters all recorded versions of the "Catfish" theme within months of each other, making it impossible to decipher the exact chronology. Nonetheless, an evolution can be observed if we take Thomas's "primitive" form of the lick as the oldest **(Fig. 1)** and based on McClennan's. Restricted to just the root (E), ♭3rd (G), and 4th (A) without any bends or pull-offs, it harkens back to the most basic accompaniment in the bluesman's key of E.

John Lee Hooker, no stranger to the more primal forms of modal Delta blues, embellishes the three main notes in **Fig. 2** with a bend from the 4th (A) to the 5th (B), followed by the pull-off to the ♭3rd (G) and resolved to the root. In addition, he drops in the lower octave E, thereby displaying almost all of the final elements. He also plays the open B string after the bend up to B as an eccentricity that his followers did not include. Like Thomas, his version also seems to be inspired by McClennan.

Muddy Waters called his second version "Still a Fool" **(Fig. 3)** and incorporated a release from the 5th to the 4th before it is pulled-off to the ♭3rd that is more pronounced than in "Rolling Stone." This needs to be executed smoothly for the best results, as you do not want to hear any hitches from the bend to the pull-off. Notice also the subtle hammer-on from the ♭7th (D) to the root following the low E on beat 1 after the pickup.

In the late '60s, Jimi Hendrix cut several versions of "Catfish Blues" as well as his original composition "Voodoo Child," which is a variation on the theme. **Fig. 4** shows how he inverted the treble and bass sections of the preceding arrangements, similar to what Muddy did on "Rolling Stone." His trill and fluid pull-off set the standard for future guitarists wishing to tap into the deep mojo associated with this hypnotic phrase.

One of the all-time great "vamps," the lick found in "Catfish Blues" provides as succinct a demonstration of classic Delta blues as you will ever find. For a good technical exercise, try playing it in keys above the open position that would require a barre with your index finger. *(Thanks to Edward Komara, the former blues archivist at the University of Mississippi, for his assistance in researching this material.)*

Fig. 1 "Catfish Blues" lick, as played by Bobo "Slim" Thomas"

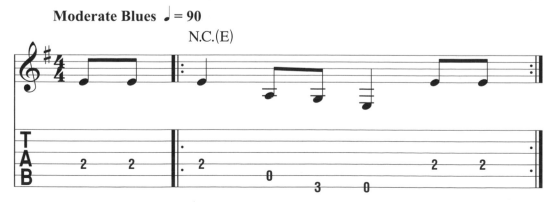

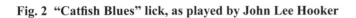

Fig. 2 "Catfish Blues" lick, as played by John Lee Hooker

Moderate Blues ♩ = 90

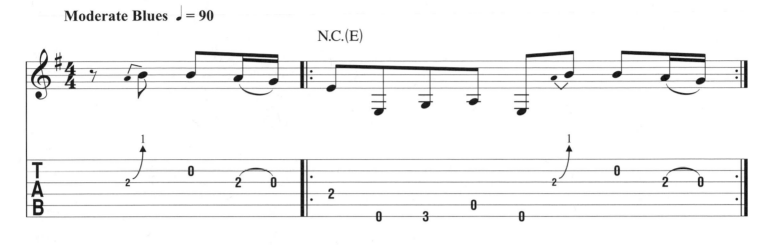

N.C.(E)

Fig. 3 "Catfish Blues" lick, as played by Muddy Waters

Slow Blues ♩ = 65 (♫ = ♪ ♪)

N.C.(E)

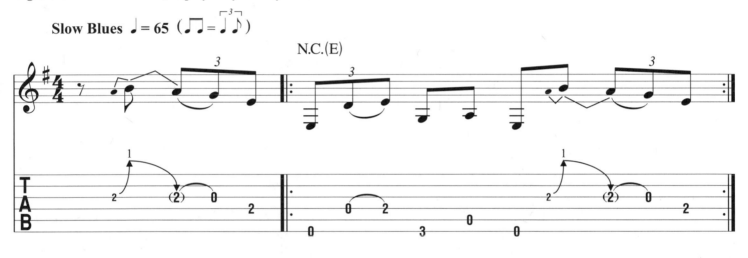

Fig. 4 "Catfish Blues" lick, as played by Jimi Hendrix

Slow Blues ♩ = 65 (♫ = ♪ ♪)

N.C.(E)

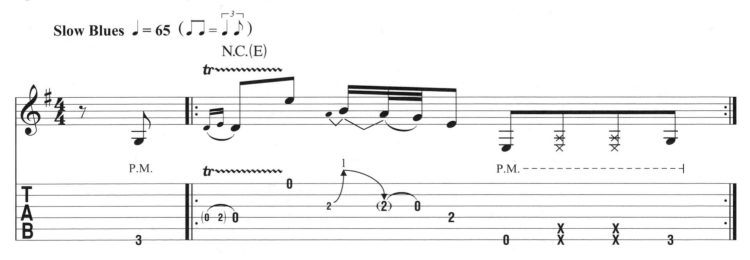

COOL BLUES

The smooth sounds of sliding 6th/9th chords

The blues is the most traditional form of American music, with sharply defined parameters and formal characteristics. Far from constricting, however, the range of expression is so expansively conceived it offers unlimited possibilities. The most evident are shuffle boogie rhythms, the blues scale, and I–IV–V chord progressions, with the latter category exhibiting countless variations based on dominant voicings. The naturally occurring dissonance between the root and ♭7th notes has come to represent the spirit of the blues, and a rich selection of hip riffs has been developed highlighting the ♭7th as well as the 6th and 9th scale degrees. Riffs combining both the 6th and 9th produce one of the most sensuous sounds available on the guitar.

Fig. 1 shows the classic, stripped-down sliding 6th/9th lick most often associated with T-Bone Walker's "Call It Stormy Monday" from 1947. Both Bone and Johnny Moore captivated club audiences in Southern California in the '40s with sophisticated 6th, 9th, and 13th chords interspersed with jazzy single-note lines. On Charles Brown's "Racetrack Blues" from 1945, Moore plays an early recorded example of this lick. Wayne Bennett graces Bobby Blue Bland's highly influential 1961 version of "Stormy Monday Blues" with several tasty variations. Observe that this slow-blues figure is especially effective when played against a second guitar or keyboard banging out dominant chords played in triplets.

One of the reasons for the demise of large horn-driven groups after World War II was the realization that electric guitars could do a credible job of filling up the harmonic space through volume and tone. Before long, inventive guitarists, especially those of the Texas variety, began replicating horn riffs to great effect. **Fig. 2** contains a rousing pattern similar to the one in Stevie Ray Vaughan's "Empty Arms" on *Soul to Soul* from 1985. As opposed to the previous figure, this sassy, serpentine example works best over a snappy shuffle beat with a second rhythm part consisting of swinging dominant chords played in quarter notes. Use your fret-hand thumb to access the bass notes, if possible, while dialing in a full, hi-fi tone with a hint of distortion for maximum impact.

Probably the coolest sliding 6th/9th riff of all is demonstrated in **Fig. 3**. Where Figs. 1 and 2 may be advanced by moving the patterns over one set of strings, Fig. 3 is at its most practical when moved up the neck in a parallel form as shown. (Note: The V chord, F7, would be played at fret 8.) Lonnie Mack, along with Michael Bloomfield, was fond of this riff and used it most expressively on "Down and Out" from *The Wham of That Memphis Man* in 1963. Make the slide on the triple stops with your index finger and catch the dyads with your pinky.

While the pursuit of hot lead licks is a worthy goal for the contemporary blues guitarist, keep in mind that it is the harmonic embellishments that provide the "bluest" characteristics of the genre. The recordings of legendary innovators such as T-Bone Walker, Johnny Moore, Gatemouth Brown, Lowell Fulson, Bill Jennings, and Billy Butler contain a wealth of material to bolster your groove.

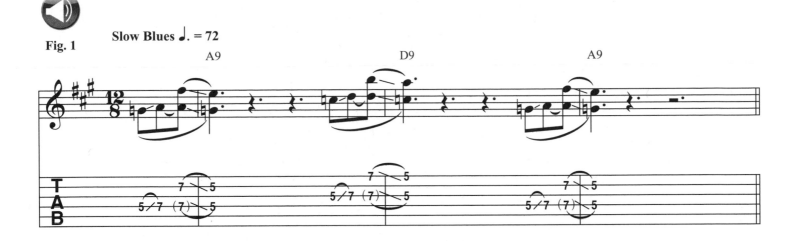

Fig. 1

Slow Blues ♩. = 72

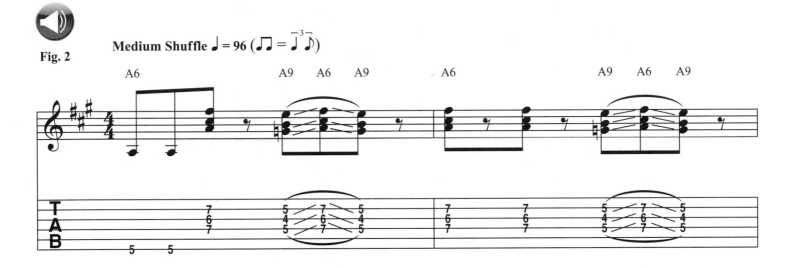

Fig. 2

Medium Shuffle ♩ = 96

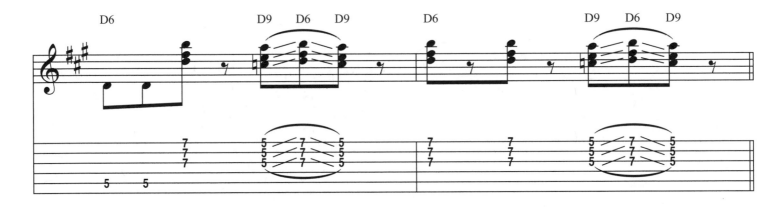

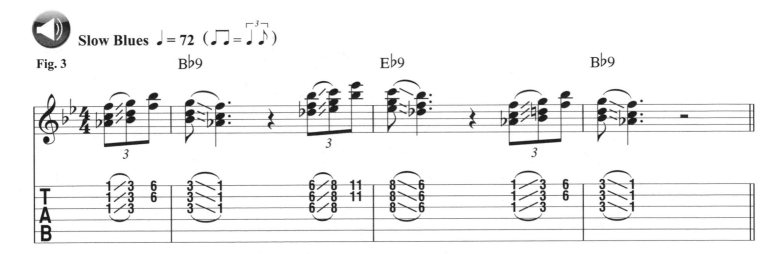

Slow Blues ♩ = 72

Fig. 3

41

COUNTRY BLUES

Accompany yourself with an authentic 12-bar pattern

Acoustic country blues was the prototype for electric blues and rock 'n' roll. Starting sometime after the Civil War, its peak period lasted from the late '20s until about 1940 in the guise of Delta blues from Mississippi. Prominent practitioners included Charley Patton, Blind Lemon Jefferson, and of course, Robert Johnson. Muddy Waters came in on the tail end of the era, taking country blues to Chicago in the mid '40s and electrifying it later in the decade.

Texas was also a fertile breeding ground for acoustic blues. One of the Lone Star state's favorite sons was Sam "Lightning" Hopkins (1912–1982). A real troubadour who could seemingly make up lyrical blues songs on the spot, Hopkins had a deceptively simple accompaniment style. As opposed to the steady, thumping 4/4 foundation underlying most Delta blues, Lightning's music often had an implied shuffle rhythm driven by boogie lines. Playing in standard tuning and mostly in the key of E, he would answer his vocal with graceful fills that did not break time.

The 12-bar blues shown in this study is a combination of Lightning's pet licks and other classic phrases inimical to the genre. While it could be executed with a flatpick, playing it fingerstyle will impart a more cohesive sound. Use your thumb for the bass notes on strings 6, 5, and 4, and a combination of your index and middle fingers for the top three strings.

The triplet figure in measures 1, 3, and 7 was a staple of Lightning's repertoire. If you slide into each one from one fret below you will impart an "organic" feel reminiscent of bottleneck guitar. John Lee Hooker was also fond of this double stop for his slow, grinding blues. In order to propel the forward momentum and maintain the impression that a loping sense of swing is underlying the entire piece, measures 2 and 4 contain basic boogie patterns. The dynamic contrast with the treble licks in measures 1 and 3 adds to the illusion of two independent guitar parts being played simultaneously throughout.

Measure 5 contains a classic country blues chord move. Based on an open position A chord, it's a slick way to change quickly from A major to A7. Barre across fret 2 with your index finger, holding down the A note on the high E string at fret 5 with your pinky. At the same time, have your middle finger in place on the G (♭7th) note at fret 3, accessing it easily by lifting your pinky off following the downstrum of the chord. Measure 6 then follows with a classic run down the E minor pentatonic scale that complements the tonality of the A7 (IV chord) while anticipating the change back to E7 (I chord) in measure 7. Resolution is particularly important in solo blues in order to maintain continuity, and is provided here by the E note on beat 4.

The "answer" phrase in measure 8 displays yet another classic lick that emphasizes the major and dominant tonality of the I chord with the major 3rd (G♯) and the ♭7th (D) notes. Compare this with the minor pentatonic scale runs in measures 6 and 10 that only contain the bluesy ♭3rd (G). The skillful mixing of minor and major 3rds is an art that country blues guitarists had to master to keep the tonality of their songs from being ambiguous while at the same time expressing the gritty, "down home" blues feel associated with the appropriate application of the ♭3rd.

Moderate Blues ♩ = 90 (♫ = ♪♪)

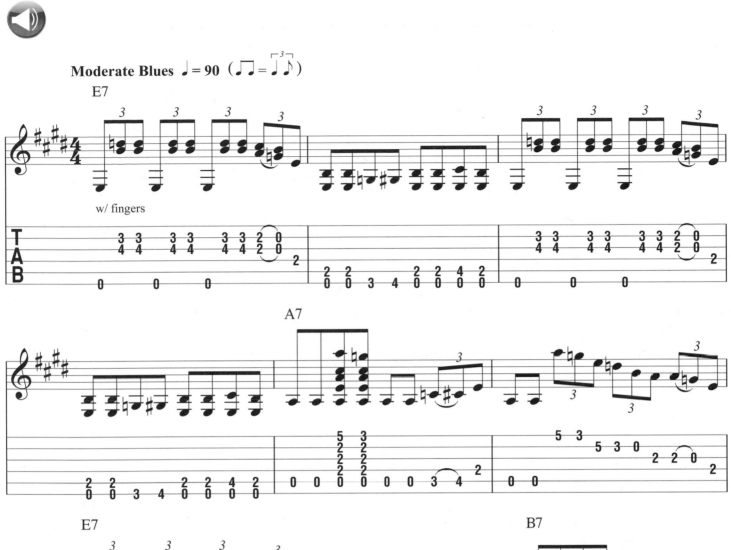

DELTA BLUES

A solo guitar accompaniment in the style of Charlie Patton, Robert Johnson, and others

Blues was played in New Orleans and other areas of the South around 1900, but its deepest roots took hold in the Mississippi Delta. Due to the area's fertile soil and access to transportation on the nearby rivers and railroads, many large plantations were located there, with equally large populations of African-American workers. Numbered among them were blues musicians whose function was to provide entertainment for the tenants. The environment was harsh, and the blues that emerged from it reflected the stark reality of everyday life.

By the early part of the century, acoustic guitars had supplanted banjos as the choice accompaniment instrument for itinerant solo performers. Charlie Patton became one of the first bluesmen in the Delta to gain notoriety on the guitar. He went on to record a number of classic blues between 1929 and 1934. Other legendary guitarists from the era of recorded Delta blues (1927–1942) were Son House, Tommy Johnson, Skip James, and, of course, Robert Johnson.

Though Delta blues guitar shares characteristics with the blues from other regions, its driving bass and hypnotic riffs separate it and give it a power that has remained undiminished through the years. The 12-bar blues example shown here is a classic illustration of Delta blues guitar. It should be played fingerstyle, with the thumb handling the bass strings, and a combination of the index and middle fingers plucking the treble strings. Notice that every measure starts with the root bass note, and is played with a shuffle rhythm to propel the progression forward. Be sure to mute strings 5 and 6 a bit throughout.

Measures 1–4 and 7–8 (I chord) contain two licks that alternate over a thumping bass pattern. In measures 1, 3, and 7, the ♭7th (D) is bent up a whole step to the root (E) followed by the open, high E string. A simple move from A (4th) to G (♭3rd) in measures 2, 4, and 6 highlights the ♭3rd, probably *the* defining scale tone of Delta blues. You should also know that the key of E was a favorite of Delta blues guitarists due to the two E strings that could drone and sustain, a necessity for achieving a full sound when accompanying oneself.

The IV (A7) chord in measures 5 and 6 is outlined succinctly with the ♭7th (G), 5th (E), and major 3rd (C♯). By the way, that quarter step bend of the G note actually places it between the ♭7th and 7th, and is known as one of the true "blue notes," along with a similar bend of the ♭3rd.

The V (B7) chord in measure 9 is approached with a smooth walk-up on beat 4 of measure 8. A standard B7 voicing is employed on beat 2, with a cool 2nd inversion (B7/F♯) appearing on beat 4. Measure 10 (IV chord) utilizes a run derived from the open, root position of the E minor pentatonic scale to add dynamics, momentum, and resolution to the turnaround (measures 11 and 12).

The turnaround consists of a bass line that implies movement from E to E7 in measure 11 and a walk-up to the V chord (B7) in measure 12.

Though composed for the acoustic guitar, like virtually all pre-war blues, this piece translates well to the electric with a touch of edgy distortion and plenty of bass. Hmm … come to think of it, that sounds like it could be a prescription for rock 'n' roll! If you don't take my word for it, just listen to Eric Clapton or any number of heavy blues-rockers.

Uptempo Blues ♩ = 120 (♫ = ♪♪³)

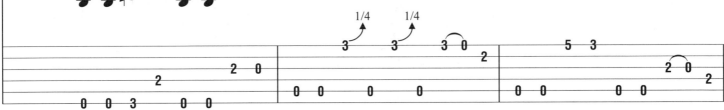

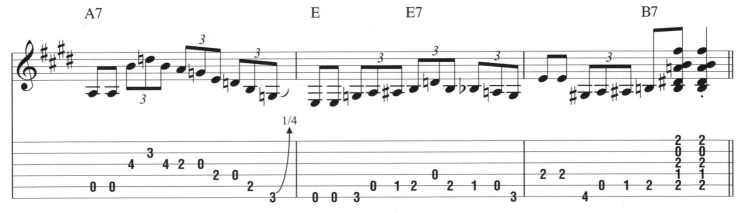

EIGHT-BAR BLUES

A variation of the standard 12-bar form

Most musicians are fondly familiar with the 12-bar blues progression and its variations. But even with four fewer measures than its 12-bar counterpart, you'll find many more variations in the eight-bar blues progression. For example, 12-bar blues progressions either begin with four measures of the I chord or with one measure of the I, one measure of the IV, and two more measures of the I. In contrast, eight-bar blues can begin with one, two, or four measures of the I chord. Even more significant is that the II, IV, V, or VI chord can follow the I, whereas in a 12-bar blues the IV chord always appears after the I chord in measure 5.

Early blues from after the Civil War through to the 1920s did not conform to one form of progression. Eight-, 12-, and 16-bar blues coexisted alongside hypnotic one-chord vamps. In addition, solo acoustic guitarists took liberties with the structures of their songs, dropping or adding measures and beats at whim to suit their vocal performances. With the development of ragtime and Dixieland music around the turn of the century adding to traditional folk and country music, however, eight-measure verses started to become the norm for American popular music.

Blues musicians would follow suit to a degree with the eight-measure form from the '20s onward. Bessie Smith waxed the classics "Tain't Nobody's Bizness If I Do" in 1923 and "Nobody Knows You When You're Down and Out" in 1929 while Louis Armstrong blew hot trumpet on "Basin Street Blues" in 1928. It would take Delta blues in the '30s, with the inestimable help of Robert Johnson and his boogie shuffles, to codify 12-bar blues for the electric post-war blues era that followed a decade later in Chicago.

Despite the pervasiveness of 12-bar blues since, an impressive body of eight-bar blues has accrued. "St. James Infirmary," "It Hurts Me, Too," "Someday After Awhile," "Hit That Highway," "Same Old Blues," "Drown in My Own Tears," "I'm Still in Love with You," "Black Magic Woman," and "Key to the Highway" are some of the most prominent.

Fig. 1 is a solo country blues excursion based on "Key to the Highway," which was written by Big Bill Broonzy and popularized by Little Walter and Eric Clapton. Observe that each chord change is harmonized with various combinations of boogie patterns, arpeggiated and strummed chords, short blues licks, and double stops. Likewise, notice that either the root note or the chord itself appears on beat 1 while beat 4 contains a bass line or pattern that leads the ear to the next change, each contributing to the structural integrity of the piece.

Fig. 2 is a more sophisticated and urbane eight-bar slow blues progression. As opposed to Fig. 1, it contains altered diatonic chords (II, III, and VI) as well as the basic I, IV, and V changes and is a fine example of the rich harmonic choices available. Notice that the D#°7 and A#°7 in measures 4 and 7 are substitutes for the D and A7 chords, respectively, and lead smoothly to the next chord change.

With their invigorating alternate chord changes, eight-bar blues offer a stimulating opportunity to stretch your harmonic knowledge. At the same time, they are terrific vehicles for improvisation. For example, try using either the F# minor pentatonic scale (F#–A–B–C#–E) or the F# Aeolian mode (F#–G#–A–B–C#–D–E) over Fig. 2 for an enjoyable learning experience.

Fig. 1

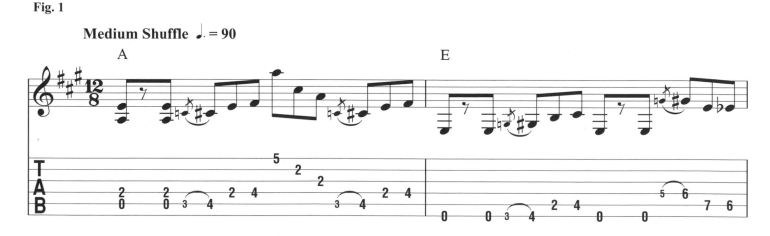

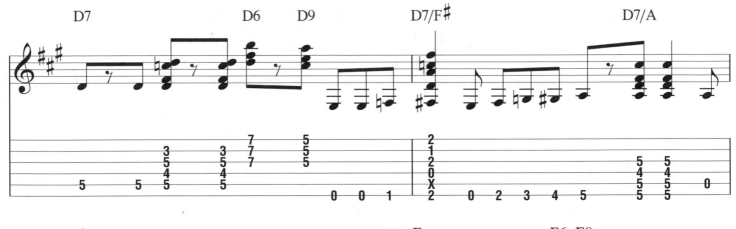

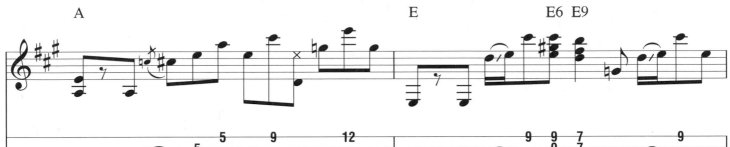

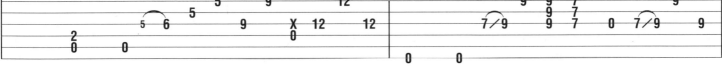

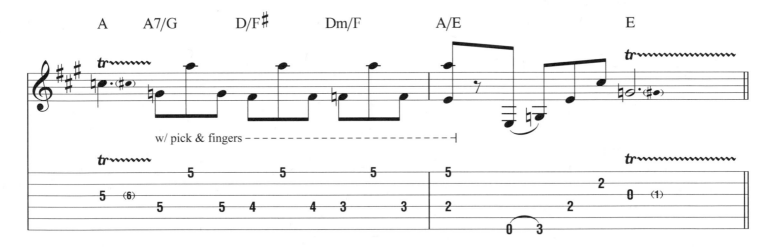

Fig. 2

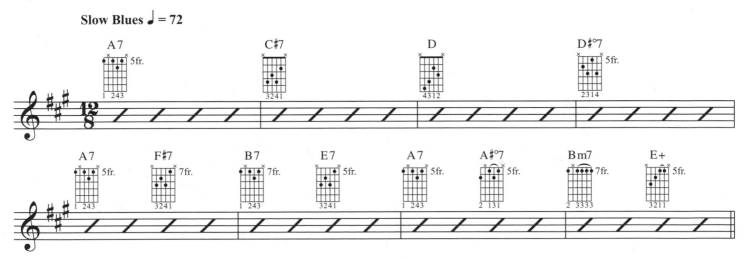

FREDDIE KING

Licks and fills in the style of the "Texas Cannonball"

He was a mountain of a man with a sound and voice to match. As one of the three "Kings" of electric blues guitar, along with B.B. and Albert, Freddie was arguably the most awesome instrumentalist of the trinity.

A proud son of the Lone Star State, Freddie moved to Chicago in the early '50s, where Jimmy Rodgers and Eddie Taylor befriended him. It was Rodgers who suggested that Freddie drop the flatpick in favor of a plastic thumbpick and a metal index fingerpick, a move that contributed to his biting attack and thumping bass-string work. He hung out and jammed with Magic Sam, Hubert Sumlin, Howlin' Wolf, Robert Lockwood, Jr., and Hound Dog Taylor, but his career remained stalled in the clubs until he relocated to Cincinnati, Ohio, in 1960. Signing with King/Federal Records, he went on to produce a spectacular number of instrumentals, including "Hide Away," "San-Ho-Zay," and "The Stumble," along with vocal standards like "Have You Ever Loved a Woman," "I'm Tore Down," "Full Time Love," and "Lonesome Whistle Blues."

His star dipped somewhat in the late '60s, only to rise again in the early '70s when he signed with Leon Russell's Shelter Records and began playing with Eric Clapton. One of his prize "pupils," Clapton introduced Freddie to an enthusiastic rock audience hungry for deep blues. Unfortunately, the rejuvenated bluesman died in 1976 at age 42, just as he was entering yet another productive phase of his career.

Two anecdotes give insight into the mind of this brilliant and competitive musician. The late Luther Allison recalled to his son Bernard that nobody ever wanted to play one of Freddie's guitars because they were strung with such heavy strings. In addition, Steady Rollin' Bob Margolin relates how Freddie always insisted on playing last at jams. After carefully listening to all the other guitarists, he would make sure to play something entirely different from everyone else.

Freddie King's guitar style could fill a book, but the following examples should give you a tantalizing taste. **Fig. 1** shows a typical opening phrase using the root position of the C blues scale that includes the 6th (A) and major 3rd (E) notes from the C Mixolydian mode. Check out the quarter step bend to the true "blue note" between the ♭3rd and 3rd on beat 4 of measure 1.

The lick in **Fig. 2** is a graceful "end" turnaround that resolves to a cool 9th voicing. The "Albert King box" is employed in **Fig. 3**, as Freddie again commandeers the ♭3rd and the major 3rd as a way of resolving to the root note in measure 3. In **Fig. 4**, tasty 6ths, a hallmark of songs like "Hide Away" and "The Stumble," are presented in the key of E. **Fig. 5** has a tangy I chord hook similar to "Wash Out." This type of hook can give your rhythm part a little extra punch, as opposed to normal blues comping patterns. **Fig. 6** provides a similar alternative for the V and IV chords.

Freddie's style was the perfect blend of virtuosity, soul, and taste. He left an unparalleled recorded legacy and was a major influence on countless guitarists including Luther Allison, Stevie Ray Vaughan, and contemporary players like Debbie Davies, Tinsley Ellis, and Jimmy Thackery.

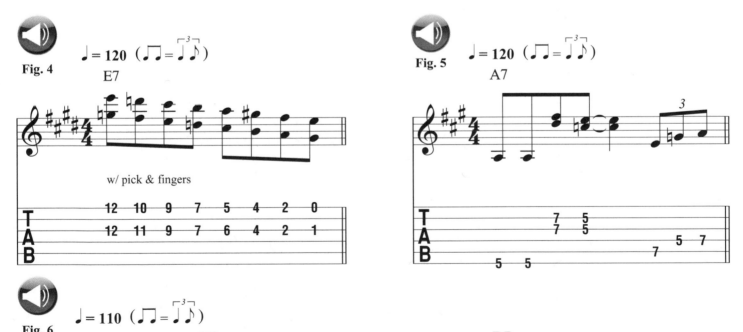

JOHN LEE HOOKER

Endless boogie

John Lee Hooker's stylistic contribution to the blues can be divided into three categories: back-snapping boogies, dark and menacing slow blues, and driving mid-tempo progressions. The "Hook" waxed poetically and powerfully in each area, but it's his starring role as the "Boogie Man" that holds the most fascination for guitarists. The Detroit bluesman (by way of the Mississippi Delta) died on June 21, 2001, but not before bestowing his special gift on the world. As he said in "Boogie Chillen #2," "When you got that boogie in you, it got to come out."

Hooker played in open G, open A, and standard tunings. Be hip that open A (E–A–E–A–C♯–E, low to high) is the same relative tuning as open G (D–G–D–G–B–D) except that the altered strings go up one step in pitch, rather than down. Most of Hooker's boogies are in the key of A, and it is possible to play them in standard tuning with no loss of effect.

Boogie woogie had deep, thick roots at the end of the 19th century in the Midwest where it was called "fast western." Originally played by groups of two or three guitar players in lumber and turpentine camps as entertainment for the laborers, it would find its greatest development in the hands of piano players. Nonetheless, guitarists like the immortal Blind Lemon Jefferson from Texas were playing moving bass lines and singing about a "booger rooger," or house party, as early as 1911. The term boogie woogie itself is attributed to Charles "Cow Cow" Davenport, who used it to describe the blues-based piano playing of Clarence "Pinetop" Smith, the artist behind the seminal "Pinetop's Boogie Woogie" from 1929.

In order to appreciate Hooker's accomplishment, dig that his landmark "Boogie Chillen" from 1948 sounds like none of the above. Played on a hollowbody guitar through a cranked, primitive tube amp, it rocks insistently with a hypnotically repetitive "hook." **Fig. 1** contains a similar pattern. To help achieve the proper rhythmic groove, try playing the bass notes with your thumb and the A triads with an upstrum of the index finger.

Fig. 2 is a bluesier riff courtesy of the ♭3rd (C) bent a quarter step to the "true blue" note between the ♭3rd and the major 3rd (C♯). Access the A note on the high E string at fret 5 with your pinky. Be aware that if Hooker were in open A tuning, all he would have to do is strum strings 5–2 open while fretting just the A note on string 1 to execute the A chord on beat 3.

Though still based around the A blues tonality, **Fig. 3** appears to have more movement via the bluesy 3rds surrounding the requisite A triads, and is related to Hooker's slow-blues excursions. Like his Texas counterpart Lightnin' Hopkins, Hook would often play a descending series of harmonized 3rds that resolve to the tonic triad or the root bass note. Observe how the chords are strummed on the upbeat, which is the "secret" to making boogies (or shuffles, in many cases) really swing.

Fig. 4 is about as close to a Chicago blues boogie bass pattern as Hooker would get.

Fig. 5 should have a familiar ring, as it has been the basis for much butt-kicking boogie rock. The inclusion of implied ♭III (C) and IV (D) chords leading to the I (A) makes for a tremendous amount of drive. ZZ Top's "La Grange," à la **Fig. 6**, and Norman Greenbaum's "Spirit in the Sky" (which reverses the ♭III and IV chords) each owe their existence to this boogie beat. As Billy Gibbons quoted Mr. Hooker, "How, how, how, how!"

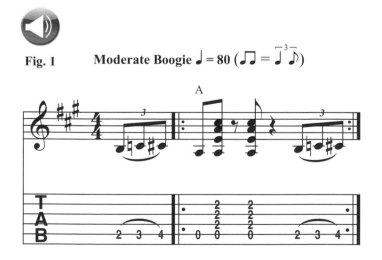

Fig. 1   Moderate Boogie ♩ = 80

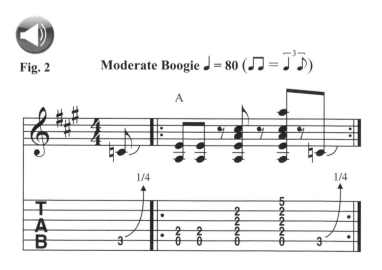

Fig. 2   Moderate Boogie ♩ = 80

JUMP BLUES

Essential elements to get you jumpin', jivin', and wailin'

As an offshoot of blues, swing, and R & B, jump blues is one of the prototypes of rock 'n' roll. Uptempo and energetic, it follows the 12-bar blues form with hot, horn-based riffs accenting the I–IV–V chord changes. The jump blues era lasted roughly a decade, between 1945 and 1955. The swing revival of the '90s, however, with bands like Big Bad Voodoo Daddy, Cherry Poppin' Daddies, and particularly the Brian Setzer Orchestra, incorporated a fair share of jitterbugging jump tunes. In addition, the West Coast bands of James Harmon, Rod Piazza, Mitch Woods, and Rick Holmstrom have regularly included an invigorating dose of the music for years.

The roots of jump blues originate with the Kansas City swing of Count Basie in the '30s, boogie-woogie piano, and country blues prior to World War II. By 1940, saxophonist/singer/frontman Louis Jordan had adapted the shuffle rhythm to swing and blues to great public acclaim. Lionel Hampton and Buddy Johnson would soon join the fun, with honking saxes and foot-stomping rhythms in their orchestras.

It would take T-Bone Walker in the mid '40s, however, to bring the guitar to the fore. "Bone" opened the door for, among countless others, Gatemouth Brown and obscure guitarists like Eddie Lambert with Chris Powell & the Five Blue Flames in the late '40s. Powell's rocking ensemble would in turn have a significant influence on Bill Haley's guitarist Danny Cedrone, who played the landmark solo on "Rock Around the Clock" in 1956.

After Ike Turner's "Rocket 88" in 1951, featuring Willie Kizart's raucous distorted guitar, the demarcations between styles became blurred, as rockabilly and then rock 'n' roll exhibited the swinging comp chords, boogie bass lines, and big back beat of jump blues. By the late '50s, R & B music was fading into doo-wop and then soul music, the wailing saxophone was supplanted by the guitar and the piano, and almost all blues-based styles had been absorbed into pop culture.

Fig. 1 shows a comp pattern familiar to jump blues that appears most prominently in "Rock Around the Clock." The melodic 6th chord as the I, as opposed to the bluesy 7th or 9th, is one of the characteristics that often differentiates jump blues from Chicago blues, for example.

The tenor sax reigned as king in jump blues. The "hooky" licks it played were often quite simple and repetitive, but very effective for capturing one's attention and filling the dance floor. **Fig. 2** employs the 5th (D), 6th (E), root (G), and 3rd (B), respectively, from the major scale over the I chord (G7). This same pattern can be employed over the IV chord (C7) by simply replacing the B note with a B♭.

As amplified guitars began substituting for horn sections and even keyboards in the '50s, guitarists found that they had to sometimes play rhythm and lead licks simultaneously to fill out the harmony. Figs. 3–4 are good examples of this in action. **Fig. 3** uses notes from the G composite blues scale (Mixolydian mode and blues scale) along with triple stops, while **Fig. 4** incorporates a boogie bass line with a 1st-inversion G9 chord.

KILLER BLUES TONES

Classic guitar/amp combos of B.B. King, Albert King, and SRV

Electric blues guitarists quickly realized that amplified instruments were not just louder, but that they produced an altogether different sound that could be incorporated into a personal style. Charlie Christian, the jazz legend and electric guitar pioneer who came from the blues, based his revolutionary improvisations on the sound and phrasing of saxophone players. In the 1940s T-Bone Walker, Christian's contemporary, also picked up on the fact that, plugged in, he could compete as a solo voice with horn players. Indeed, his sophisticated rhythm work demonstrated that one person comping on the electric guitar could easily fill the sonic space occupied by an entire horn section.

In 1948, when Muddy Waters and John Lee Hooker recorded the epochal "I Can't Be Satisfied" and "Boogie Chillun," respectively, the "tone" was set for postwar blues and the rock 'n' roll that would follow in the 1950s. Crackling with natural tube-amp distortion, the thrilling sound of these classics would help provide the impetus for B.B. King to explore the expressive possibilities of sustain, thereby influencing virtually every electric guitarist in his wake.

Though he has had many different "Lucilles" in his arms since the late '40s, B.B. has come to be associated most with the thinline, semi-hollow ES-335, -345, and -355 series from Gibson that debuted in 1958. On *Live at the Regal*, his spectacular live set from 1965, he plays a fancy, circa 1963 ES-355 through a pre-CBS Fender Twin. Along with the substantial volume of the vintage tube amp, B.B.'s habit of having both humbucking pickups on (without engaging the Varitone, Vibrola, or stereo capabilities of the 355) and blending them together produces his warm, round tone with a hint of "bite."

Fig. 1 shows a sample of his playing from this period of his career. Adding in the major 3rd (E) and 6th (A) from the C composite blues scale (a combination of the blues scale and the major pentatonic scale), he also bends the ♭3rd (E♭) up a 1/4 step to the "true blue note" in measure 2 before kicking it up the extra semitone to the melodic major 3rd (E), thereby releasing the musical tension.

Albert King was already sporting his signature 1958 Gibson Flying V when he signed with Stax Records in 1966. By the time he cut the epochal *Born Under a Bad Sign* a year later he was achieving a huge sound (to match his physical presence) by playing through a solid-state (!) Acoustic 270 head and cabinet (with a high-frequency horn) that, amazingly, pumped out tons of bass. The high-output PAF humbucking pickups of the V and Albert's use of his thumb added considerable warmth and fatness to the cooler sound of the transistor amp.

Fig. 2 is a tasty example of the "Albert King box" and his slinky bending technique. Though transcribed in standard tuning, be hip that the "Velvet Bulldozer" employed an unorthodox tuning (low to high: C–F–C–F–A–D) along with custom strings gauged .050, .038, .028, and .024 (wound) on the bottom, with super-light .012 and .009 (unwound) strings on top.

Stevie Ray Vaughan was a confirmed Strat-slinger like one of his idols, Jimi Hendrix. His 1959 "Number 1" with the rosewood fingerboard and reversed whammy-bar block was strung with knuckle-busting .013-.056 gauge strings, though he did tune down a half step to ease the Olympic archery tension. Stevie was all over the board with various amps, but did have a passion for pre-CBS Fender Vibroverbs and Ibanez TS-8 and TS-9 Tube Screamers. **Fig. 3** spotlights his vaunted proficiency in the open position of E as found on *Texas Flood* from 1983.

The prevailing wisdom is that one's sound ultimately emanates from the fingers, but finding a guitar/amp combination that speaks to your soul should not be casually dismissed. In addition, be aware that other fine artists like Elmore James, Jimmy Reed, and Hubert Sumlin often played budget Harmony, National, and Silvertone guitars for a rugged, funky tone.

Fig. 1 B.B. King

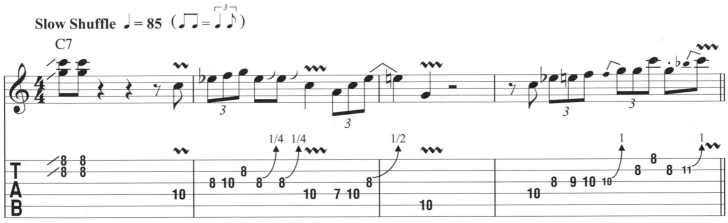

Fig. 2 Albert King

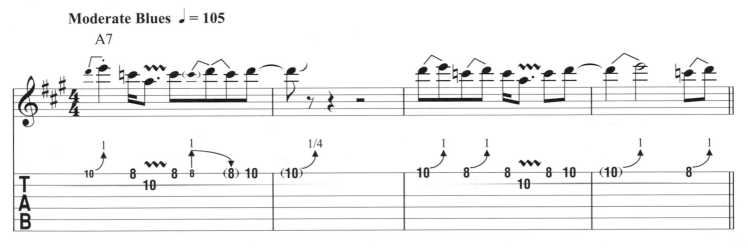

Fig. 3 Stevie Ray Vaughan

MEMPHIS SOUL

The rhythm guitar style of soul legend Steve Cropper

It's unlikely that many people who watched the Blues Brothers in the late '70s on *Saturday Night Live* realized who John Belushi was talking to when he turned to the guitar player in the band and said, "Play it, Steve." Though hardly qualified, comedians Belushi and Dan Aykroyd were standing in front of none other than soul guitarist extraordinaire Steve Cropper and bassist Donald "Duck" Dunn from Booker T. & the MGs, as well as blues guitar legend Matt "Guitar" Murphy and a selection of top New York studio cats. Purists howled, but the gig and resulting #1 album, *Briefcase Full of Blues*, served to thrust Cropper and company into the spotlight and provide a steady gig.

Steve "The Colonel" Cropper formed a high school blues and rock 'n' roll band that became the Mar-Keys around 1960 and released the seminal R & B instrumental "Last Night" in 1961. The surprise hit paved the way for a future classic, "Green Onions," in 1962 with the interracial instrumental group that would become Booker T. & the MGs. That same year, Stax Records was formed, and Cropper became musical director. Stax was the Southern soul label with Steve writing, playing, and producing for some of the biggest stars of the genre. Songs such as "I Can't Turn You Loose," "I've Been Loving You Too Long," "Dock of the Bay" with Otis Redding, "Midnight Hour" with Wilson Pickett, "Soul Man" and "Hold On, I'm Coming" with Sam & Dave, and "Knock on Wood" with Eddie Floyd are just some of the perennial standards waxed in that golden era.

When Stax Records folded in the early '70s, Cropper went on to produce for other artists, including Jeff Beck, Ringo Starr, and Buddy Guy. Though the MGs officially disbanded with the demise of Stax, they have reunited several times over the years and were inducted into the Rock and Roll Hall of Fame in 1992. Cropper continues playing and working full time at his studio in Nashville as well as with his own record label, Play It, Steve Records.

Cropper is the master of the understated fill, supportive rhythm accompaniment, and chordal hook. **Fig. 1** shows an intro or bridge with 6ths in the manner of "Soul Man," The glisses impart an organic quality that derives from the blues of T-Bone Walker and adds rhythmic and harmonic variety to the static G harmony. The melodic bass line (played by the bass and guitar in unison) in **Fig. 2** is based on "I Can't Turn You Loose."

Rufus Thomas had a hit with "Walkin' the Dog" in 1963, thanks in part to a greasy C Mixolydian riff provided by Cropper similar to the one in **Fig. 3**. **Fig. 4** is like "Tramp" by Lowell Fulson and displays the upper-register triadic forms (from the harmonized C major scale) that Cropper often favored in order to complement the rhythm section without intruding on the sonic space covered by the keyboards. The grittier side of the tasty instrumentals purveyed by Booker T. & the MGs in tunes like "Boot-Leg" is contained in the bluesy hook of **Fig. 5**.

Though he is a powerful soloist, Steve Cropper has always sublimated the impulse to play flash guitar in favor of adding the perfect rhythm part or embellishment. Learn to incorporate some of his choice ideas, and discover the joy of playing "inside" the song.

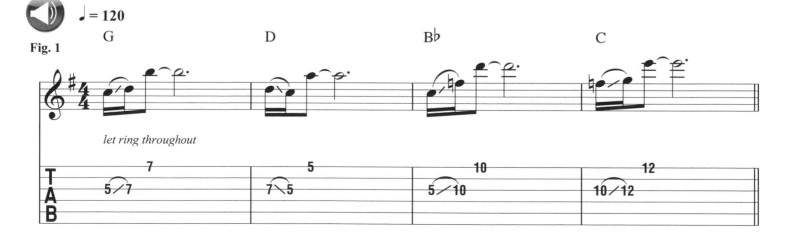

Fig. 1 ♩ = 120

Fig. 2 ♩ = 130

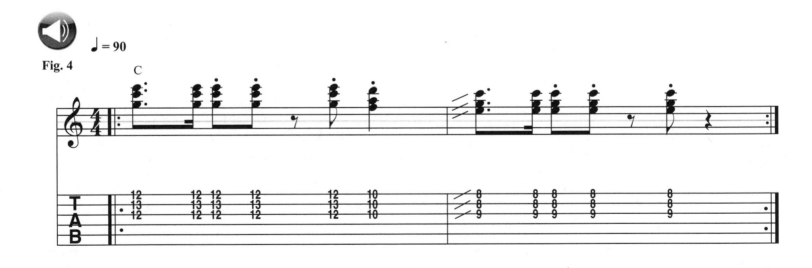

Fig. 3 ♩ = 120

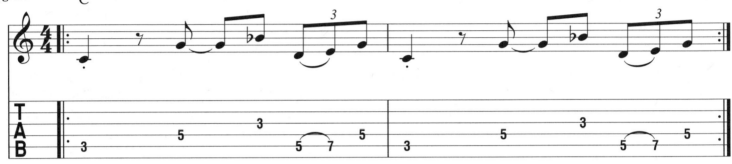

Fig. 4 ♩ = 90

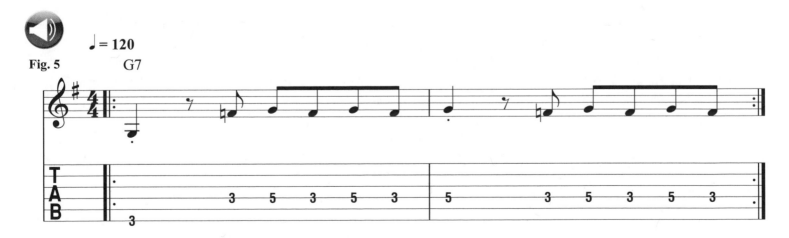

Fig. 5 ♩ = 120

MINOR BLUES

Get out of your major rut!

Most blues are in a major key. Due to the prominent inclusion of the ♭3rd (or "minor") note from the blues scale in the riffs and solos, however, a "major/minor ambiguity" is often present in major-key blues that results in a somber, melancholy feeling. Long considered the defining quality of slow blues and a sonority to be nurtured and cultivated, it permeates minor-key blues via minor chord progressions.

In major key blues, the I, IV, and V chords are always a combination of dominant 7th, 9th, or 13th chords, along with the occasional major triad. In minor key blues there are three ways to arrange the I–IV–V chord changes:

1) i=minor, IV=dominant, V=dominant

2) i=minor, iv=minor, V=dominant

3) i=minor, iv=minor, v=minor

The history of minor key blues extends all the way back to the first published blues by W. C. Handy. "St. Louis Blues" from 1914 has a 16-measure third verse that modulates to Gm from G major in the previous verses. Likewise, "St. James Infirmary," another classic blues with a lyric theme that goes back hundreds of years, is an eight-measure minor key blues. And yet, except for Skip James, who literally played in an open minor tuning a great deal of the time, country and Delta blues artists of the '20s and '30s rarely composed in a minor key. It would take the advent of postwar Chicago blues for the minor variety to become an established part of the canon.

"All Your Love" by Magic Sam from 1957 is based on arrangement #1 above. "All Your Love (I Miss Loving)," recorded by Otis Rush in 1958, contains "rhumba-rhythm" verses that are in the arrangement of #3, along with a major key solo section and chorus. His chilling "Double Trouble" from the same year follows arrangement #2.

Sam and Rush, along with Buddy Guy, were the leading proponents of the "West Side sound" that emanated from the teeming clubs and lounges in the '50s and '60s. In contrast to the harmonica-driven South-Side blues of Muddy Waters, for instance, the West Siders were partial to minor key tonalities and the fluid solo style of B.B. King.

Though minor blues progressions from the era tend to be straightforward affairs, there is much room for variation within the confines of the harmonic progression. Led Zeppelin, with "Since I've Been Loving You" from *Led Zeppelin III* (Atlantic) in 1970, for example, expanded upon the basic i, iv, and v chords with relative-major chord substitutions and a jazzy turnaround.

The 12-bar progression shown in **Fig. 1**, which relates to arrangement #3, likewise incorporates several substitutions and additional chord voicings to provide a rich foundation upon which to build an improvisation. Measures 3–4 and 7–8 contain the same four-chord sequence that advances the progression with a chromatic bass line that descends on string 4 from chord to chord. Pop standards like "In a Sentimental Mood," "Town Without Pity," and Stevie Wonder's "Don't You Worry 'Bout a Thing" from 1973 all utilize this dramatic motif.

Measures 5–6, where the iv usually occurs, includes the v as a substitution following the iv, and the F as the relative major of Dm, which is then repeated in measure 10. Notice how the F in measure 12 leads smoothly from the Dm in measure 11 while also functioning as the ♯V resolving to the V7 (E7).

For improvisational purposes, the A minor pentatonic scale (A–C–D–E–G) will suffice. However, to do justice to the melodic possibilities inherent in the progression, the A Aeolian mode (the relative minor of C major, the key signature of the progression) in **Fig. 2** is dandy.

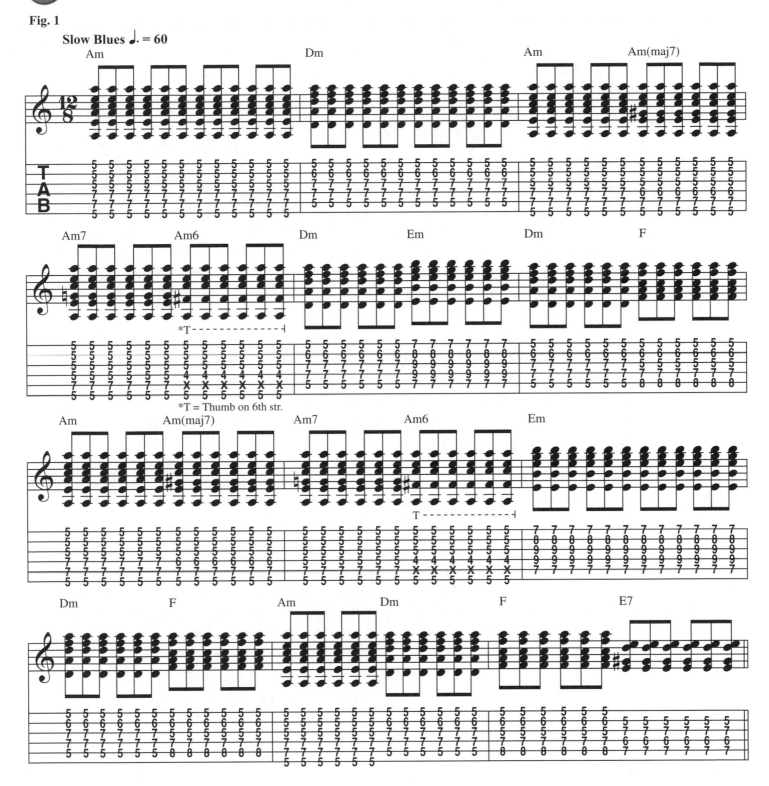

Fig. 1

Slow Blues ♩. = 60

Fig. 2

A Aeolian Mode

OPEN-STRING TURNAROUNDS

Authentic cadences for true blues power

The bodacious Billy F. Gibbons of ZZ Top once said that accurate string bending separated real blues guitarists from poseurs. The same could be said for the art of the blues turnaround. Typically occurring in the last two measures of an 8-, 12-, or 16-bar blues, it's the moment in the progression when all the improvisational information presented previously can be given a structured conclusion.

It is not certain when chord turnarounds first appeared in the blues. However, "Dallas Blues" from 1912, one of the earliest published blues, moves from the I chord to the V chord in measures 11 and 12. With the beginning of commercial recordings in the '20s, country blues guitarists started to incorporate patterns with single notes, double stops, and chord partials to imply movement from the I to the V (or I to I in some cases) at the end verses. By 1935, broken-chord patterns were common in blues, like "Farewell to You Baby" by Carl Martin (similar to Fig. 2). With the emergence of electric Chicago blues in the postwar years, structured turnarounds became a common and accepted component of the music.

Open-string turnarounds in the keys of E, A, and D were likely the first developed and are a fine place to begin your study. **Fig. 1** is no doubt the most used in the key of E and shows up regularly in the music of Muddy Waters (e.g., "I Feel Like Going Home" and "Walking Blues").

Fig. 2 is the inverse of Fig. 1, with the notes from string 5 (D, D♭, and C) appearing on string 2 and string 1 played open as a pedal tone, adding some shimmer on top for a full, ringing effect. The implied 9th chords in measure 2 maintain their voicings on strings 1–3 for a seamless transition as well as a touch of sophistication. Check out Robert Johnson's "Sweet Home Chicago" (1936) for a creative variation on this theme.

Open-string bass lines have been a characteristic of country blues turnarounds at least since Blind Lemon Jefferson skillfully wove them into his virtuosic numbers in the mid '20s. **Fig. 3** is remarkable for its utter simplicity along with the efficiency with which it moves from I to V, as measure 1 literally contains every note from the E blues scale (E–G–A–B♭–B–D). Observe the substitution of the major 3rd (G♯) in measure 2 to imply E major before the resolution to the V chord. Lightnin' Hopkins, another legendary Texas guitarist like Lemon, played patterns similar to these on tunes like "Dirty House Blues" from 1952.

The key of D is often associated with slide in open D tuning and **Fig. 4** is reminiscent of what you might hear Elmore James play on any of his classics (e.g., "Dust My Broom"). The addition of the 5th (A) on string 3 requires precise fingering in order to execute the pattern smoothly. Start with your middle finger on the A note and then add your pinky to the D note on string 2. Use your ring finger to begin the descending bass line on fret 3, followed by your index finger on frets 2 and 1.

SLOW 12/8

Type 1

Like gender, there are two main types of 12-bar blues progressions. Type 1 begins with four measures of the I chord, advancing to the IV chord in measures 5 and 6. This is often referred to as the "slow change," in musician's parlance. Dig that, like the sexes, there are some 12-bar progressions that vary from the norm—but more on that later (substitutions on the 12-bar blues, not the gender benders!).

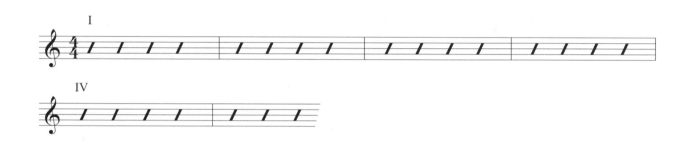

Because those four measures of the I chord can drag by at tempos below 80 bpm, most slow blues follow the type 2 arrangement (the "fast change"—see page 64). Nevertheless, a musically hypnotic effect can be engendered by maintaining the I chord for four long measures. B.B. King's "When My Heart Beats Like a Hammer" (1954) is one of the classic slow blues that fits this category.

Four-note chords are typical of Chicago and Texas electric blues. The G7 form is known as a "dead-string" chord thanks to the muting of string 5.

It's a richer and more pronounced dominant voicing—due to the interval of a ♭7th (G to F) between strings 6 and 4—than the standard "E-form" barre chord G7 with the interval of a 5th (G to D) on the bottom two strings.

Be aware that you could add the 5th to the top of the ninth chords (C9 and D9) by continuing the barre with your ring finger across strings 3 and 2 to string 1. In fact, this is done here on the last D9 chord of the turnaround.

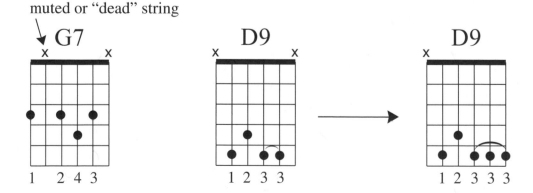

Type 2

The vast majority of slow drags are like type 2, the "fast change." A whole book could be devoted to songs that fall neatly into this pattern. These would include popular standards like T-Bone Walker's "Stormy Monday" (1947), B.B. King's "Sweet Little Angel" (1956), Larry Davis's "Texas Flood" (1958), and Freddie King's "Have You Ever Loved a Woman" (1960).

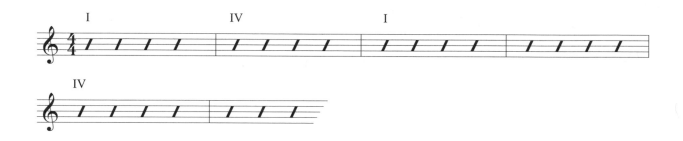

It is easy to see why the type 2 slow blues progression is favored over type 1. The increased harmonic movement maintains momentum (I to IV is the most powerful chord change in music) while providing more melodic possibilities for the singer and instrumentalists. In addition, because the change from I to IV creates tension that is released by resolving back to the I, an extra opportunity for this dramatic chord shift occurs.

Savor the darker chord voicings in Figure 2. These add drama, as well as a fat, full sound. Note also the use of second inversions (the 5th on the bottom, instead of the root or 3rd) in measures 2, 4, 8, 11, and 12. Is it not cool how the common tone (A) between the A7 and D7/A facilitates a smooth transition? The same hip move happens between measures 8 (A7/E) and 9 (E7). A logical fingering pattern will follow if you use your middle finger for the lowest note in each of these voicings. This approach should also be applied to the A7 (meas. 1, 3, 7, 11, and 12) along with the E7 (meas. 9) and D7 (meas. 10).

A relatively "clean" tone (such as what Robert Cray normally utilizes) is suggested when playing these "bassy" chords. Too much distortion will choke your sound, as sure as fast fried food will clog your arteries.

Fig. 2

Slow Blues ♩. = 62

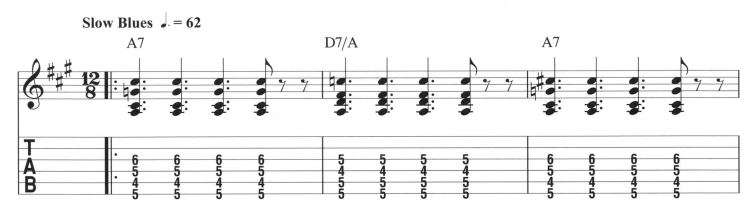

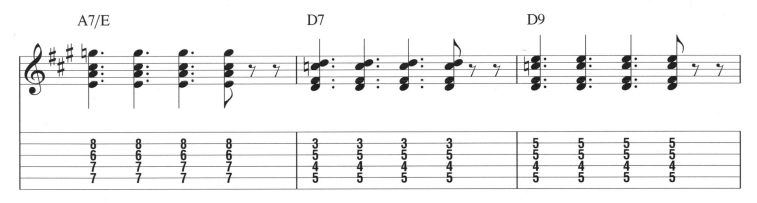

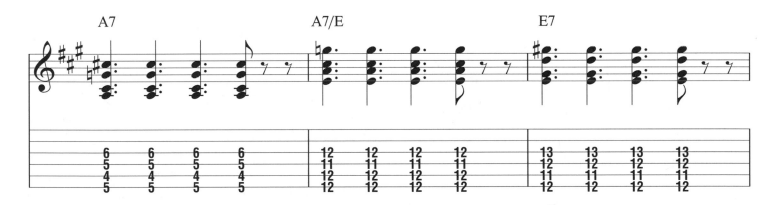

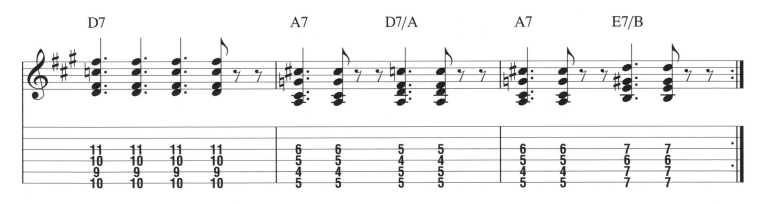

SOLO ACOUSTIC BLUES, CHICAGO STYLE!

From Mississippi to the Windy City

When Muddy Waters hauled his rough-and-tumble electrified blues out of the South Side Chicago clubs and into the Chess studios in 1948, it was a bold and visionary move. Indeed, the wedding of primitive amplification to country blues produced a revolutionary sound that not only helped to usher in the age of postwar electric blues (John Lee Hooker was concurrently doing his boogie in Detroit), but foresaw the development of rock 'n' roll as well. Muddy's little overdriven amps produced a thick, vibrant sound that allowed emphasis in the lower registers previously unattainable with acoustic guitars.

Nonetheless, the framework and forms for this new music were the acoustic country blues that he and his friendly (?) rival Howlin' Wolf had played in the Delta a decade earlier. In particular, Muddy's historic recordings by Alan Lomax for the Library of Congress in 1941 to 1942 provided material for his landmark Chess sides "I Can't Be Satisfied" and "I Feel Like Going Home." Though he never bumped into him (at the "crossroads" or anywhere else), Muddy always credited Robert Johnson with being the main inspiration for his deep blues via Son House. Charlie Patton, the "Founder of the Delta Blues," would also have to be included as a primary source, as he was for Howlin' Wolf.

Artists like Taj Mahal and John Hammond, Jr. have included elements of Chicago blues in their solo acoustic stylings over the years. Possibly the greatest example, however, is to be found on Muddy Waters' *Folk Singer* album from 1963 with Willie Dixon on doghouse bass, drummer Clifton James, and a young, energetic Buddy Guy on flat-top acoustic guitar. Hoping to capitalize on the folk boom of the early '60s, when sales of blues records were starting to slide before the coming Blues Revival, the Chess brothers were attempting to position Muddy for the college crowd. Of course, the aural results were pure down-home blues filtered through a Chicago blues sensibility, courtesy of the rhythm section and Buddy's "modern" improvisations.

The following music example is a fingerstyle 12-bar blues verse played in the solo acoustic Chicago blues style and featuring

a number of salient characteristics. Measures 1–4 show a favorite device that Muddy nicked from RJ for adding perceived harmonic movement to what is essentially four measures of the I (E7) chord. Note that the E°7 chord could also imply the IV chord as an A7♭9 (E=5th, G=♭7th, B♭=♭9th, and C♯/D♭=3rd) if the progression had the "quick change" in measure 2 indicated by the open A string.

Check out the classic hammer-on from the minor 3rd (G) to the major 3rd (G♯) in measure 4 (and measures 7, 11, and 12) that defines the major tonality of the I chord. The fill in measure 6 (IV chord) made its rounds in Chi-Town in the '50s and '60s, and has a pedigree running back through B.B. King and earlier. Dig that the scale from which it is derived could be seen as the A Mixolydian mode (with an added ♭9th) or the E composite blues scale (combination of E blues and E Mixolydian). The root note (open string) again provides the context.

Measure 7 (I chord) sports a "hooky" pattern similar to Muddy's "Hoochie Coochie Man" and "Mannish Boy," and sets up the "response" to the "call" with the "spiky" fill in measure 8. Along with the run down the A Mixolydian mode in measure 10 (IV chord), it illustrates an example of the lead style favored by Jimmy Rogers, among others. Measure 11 (I chord), the first bar of the turnaround, incorporates the D/B (♭7th and 5th, respectively) double stop that is a cornerstone of the "Chicago sound" and boots the progression forward through the energy of the triplets.

Performance Tip: Use your pick-hand thumb for the bass notes on strings 5 and 6, and a combination of your index and middle fingers for the other strings. The chords in measures 1, 2, 3, and 5 should be strummed with an upstroke of the index or middle finger while the thumb simultaneously plucks downward.

Like all blues, the rhythm and feel is of primary importance in this piece. Make the bass notes snap and the triplets pop while imagining the whole production propelled by a diesel locomotive chugging across the prairie toward the Windy City.

Moderate Shuffle ♩ = 90 (♫ = ♩³♪)

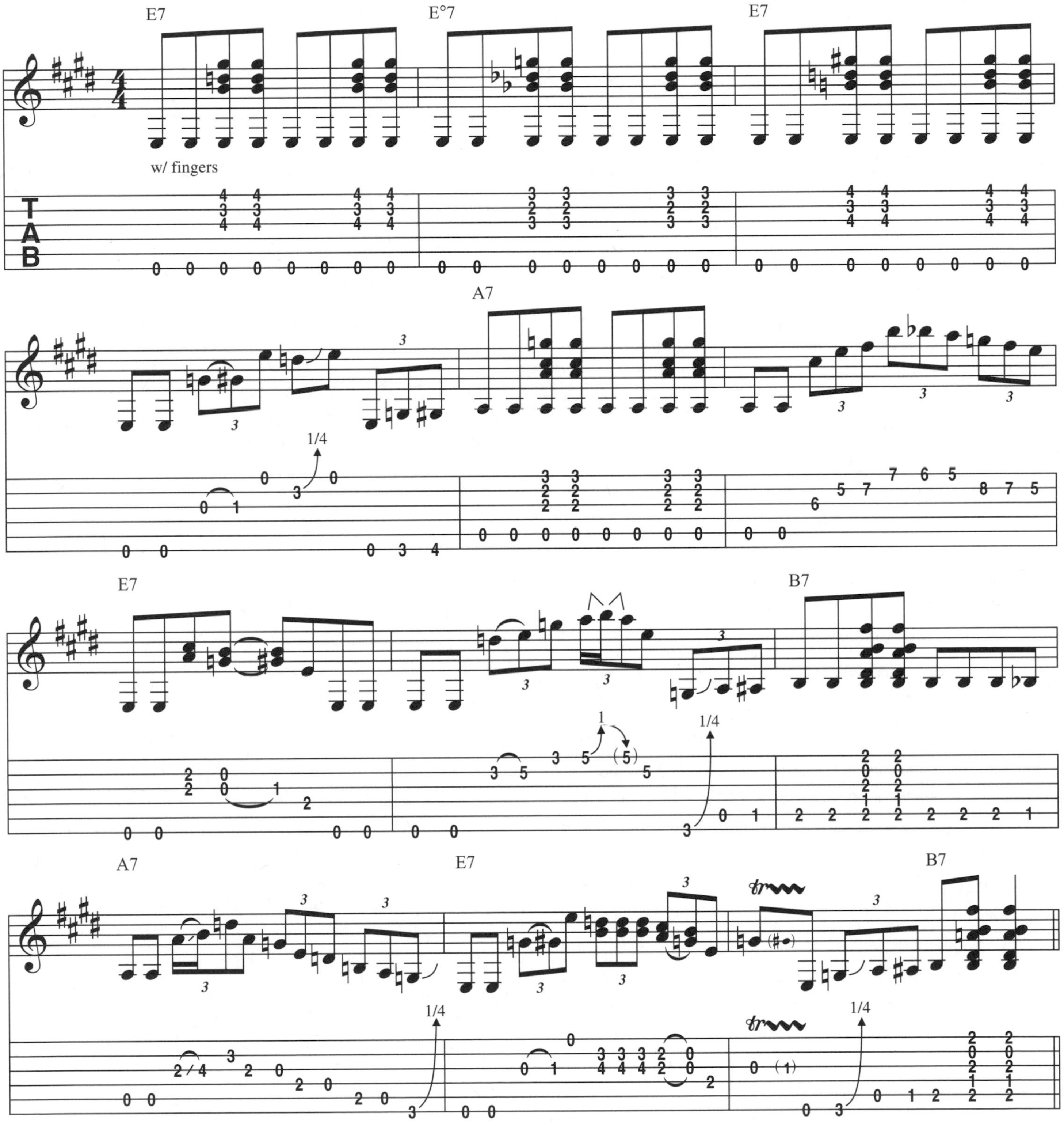

T-BONE WALKER

The father of electric blues guitar

Aaron Thibeaux "T-Bone" Walker epitomized all that is cool about the blues. Dressed to the nines in zoot suit and snappy two-tone shoes, he tossed out lyrical lead lines while holding the guitar behind his head and doing the splits. Raising himself back up, he would adjust his big hollowbody axe so that it jutted out away from his body at a rakish angle as he comped jazz chords and deftly picked over the blues scale. Though scholars continue to debate whether he, Eddie Durham, or Charlie Christian was the first to play amplified, when in fact, it was George Barnes, there can be no doubt that he was the first blues guitarist to grasp the potential of the electric guitar as a solo instrument in the early '40s. His robust tone, swinging, economical phrasing, and innovative use of the Mixolydian mode made him a match for the raspy sax players in his back-up bands, while fellow guitarists were put on notice and quickly got their chops together. Since then, virtually every electric guitarist across the board has absorbed key elements of his style.

Walker was born in Oak Cliff, Texas on May 28, 1910. His first record, "Wichita Falls Blues"/"Trinity River Blues," was cut in 1929 on an acoustic guitar in Texas, but by 1934, he was tired of the wild West and headed for the promised land of Southern California. He began performing as a singer and dancer and, around 1940, started woodshedding on the electric guitar. Walker debuted his intoxicating and lush new sound in 1942 with "I Got a Break Baby"/"Mean Old World," and a vital era in American music had arrived. From then until the mid '50s, he created a formidable body of classic blues, including the eminent "Call It Stormy Monday" in 1947. T-Bone was active both on records and in concert until his death on March 16, 1975 in Los Angeles.

The fabulous T-Bone was a complete musician. Besides composing and singing his own songs, he was an awesome rhythm guitarist, capable of driving a big band, as well as being a consummate soloist. **Fig. 1** shows a typical intro with his patented descending 9th chords and implied 13th chord extensions. The resolution to the G+, a substitute for the V chord, is a nice touch that he employed regularly.

Johnny Moore, the jazzy blues guitarist with Charles Brown, may have preceded Walker in the use of sliding 6/9 chords, but 'Bone popularized them in "Call It Stormy Monday." **Fig. 2** contains double stop forms in 6ths that outline I–IV–I changes, leading to a classic root-position lick ending on the ♭7th.

Chuck Berry is the most prominent protégé of Walker's to make the dynamic lick in **Fig. 3** his signature. Note that Chuck usually bent the 4th up to the 5th on string 3, rather than sliding up to it. This phrase works well over the I, IV, or V chord and is quite effective when repeated for a number of measures (and chord changes) to create musical tension.

Fig. 4 displays Walker's skillful blending of the basic blues scale and the Mixolydian mode into a composite blues scale. Notice the subtle bending of the 9th (A) to the ♭3rd (B♭) on string 1, and the ♭3rd on string 3 up a quarter step to the true "blue note" between the ♭3rd and the major 3rd (B).

T-Bone Walker was not only the father of electric blues guitar but also one of the most expressive and influential artists ever. His music is a constant and timeless source of inspiration for all guitarists. Even if you don't want to engage in his showmanship, incorporating the basics of T-Bone's style into your playing will benefit you enormously.

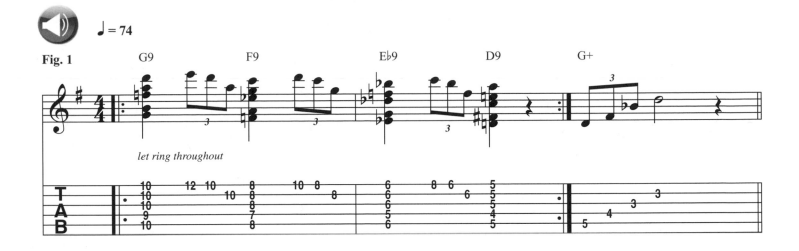

Fig. 1

let ring throughout

Fig. 2

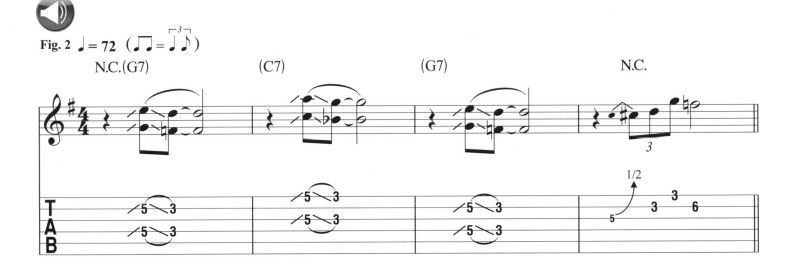

Fig. 3

Fig. 4

GUITAR NOTATION LEGEND

Guitar music can be notated three different ways: on a *musical staff*, in *tablature*, and in *rhythm slashes*.

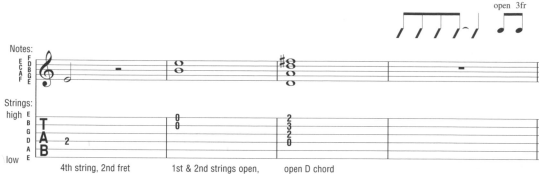

RHYTHM SLASHES are written above the staff. Strum chords in the rhythm indicated. Use the chord diagrams found at the top of the first page of the transcription for the appropriate chord voicings. Round noteheads indicate single notes.

THE MUSICAL STAFF shows pitches and rhythms and is divided by bar lines into measures. Pitches are named after the first seven letters of the alphabet.

TABLATURE graphically represents the guitar fingerboard. Each horizontal line represents a string, and each number represents a fret.

HALF-STEP BEND: Strike the note and bend up 1/2 step.

WHOLE-STEP BEND: Strike the note and bend up one step.

GRACE NOTE BEND: Strike the note and immediately bend up as indicated.

SLIGHT (MICROTONE) BEND: Strike the note and bend up 1/4 step.

BEND AND RELEASE: Strike the note and bend up as indicated, then release back to the original note. Only the first note is struck.

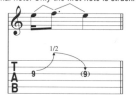

PRE-BEND: Bend the note as indicated, then strike it.

VIBRATO: The string is vibrated by rapidly bending and releasing the note with the fretting hand.

WIDE VIBRATO: The pitch is varied to a greater degree by vibrating with the fretting hand.

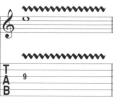

HAMMER-ON: Strike the first (lower) note with one finger, then sound the higher note (on the same string) with another finger by fretting it without picking.

PULL-OFF: Place both fingers on the notes to be sounded. Strike the first note and without picking, pull the finger off to sound the second (lower) note.

LEGATO SLIDE: Strike the first note and then slide the same fret-hand finger up or down to the second note. The second note is not struck.

SHIFT SLIDE: Same as legato slide, except the second note is struck.

TRILL: Very rapidly alternate between the notes indicated by continuously hammering on and pulling off.

TAPPING: Hammer ("tap") the fret indicated with the pick-hand index or middle finger and pull off to the note fretted by the fret hand.

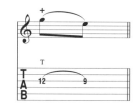

NATURAL HARMONIC: Strike the note while the fret-hand lightly touches the string directly over the fret indicated.

PINCH HARMONIC: The note is fretted normally and a harmonic is produced by adding the edge of the thumb or the tip of the index finger of the pick hand to the normal pick attack.

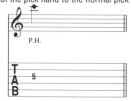

PICK SCRAPE: The edge of the pick is rubbed down (or up) the string, producing a scratchy sound.

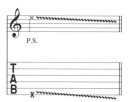

MUFFLED STRINGS: A percussive sound is produced by laying the fret hand across the string(s) without depressing, and striking them with the pick hand.

PALM MUTING: The note is partially muted by the pick hand lightly touching the string(s) just before the bridge.

RAKE: Drag the pick across the strings indicated with a single motion.

TREMOLO PICKING: The note is picked as rapidly and continuously as possible.

VIBRATO BAR DIVE AND RETURN: The pitch of the note or chord is dropped a specified number of steps (in rhythm), then returned to the original pitch.

VIBRATO BAR SCOOP: Depress the bar just before striking the note, then quickly release the bar.

VIBRATO BAR DIP: Strike the note and then immediately drop a specified number of steps, then release back to the original pitch.

MASTER THE Blues

With guitar instruction from Hal Leonard
All books include notes and tab.

Hal Leonard Guitar Method – Blues Guitar
by Greg Koch

The complete guide to learning blues guitar uses real blues songs to teach you the basics of rhythm and lead blues guitar in the style of B.B. King, Buddy Guy, Eric Clapton, and many others. Lessons include: 12-bar blues; chords, scales and licks; vibrato and string bending; riffs, turnarounds, and boogie patterns; and more!
00697326 Book/CD Pack $16.99

Blues Deluxe
by Dave Rubin

Not only does this deluxe edition provide accurate transcriptions of ten blues classics plus performance notes and artist bios, it also includes a CD with the *original Alligator Records recordings* of every song! Tunes: Are You Losing Your Mind? (Buddy Guy) • Don't Take Advantage of Me (Johnny Winter) • Gravel Road (Magic Slim) • Somebody Loan Me a Dime (Fenton Robinson) • and more.
00699918 Book/CD Pack $24.99

Art of the Shuffle
by Dave Rubin

This method book explores shuffle, boogie and swing rhythms for guitar. Includes tab and notation, and covers Delta, country, Chicago, Kansas City, Texas, New Orleans, West Coast, and bebop blues. Also includes audio for demonstration of each style and to jam along with.
00695005 Book/CD Pack $19.95

Power Trio Blues
by Dave Rubin

This book/CD pack details how to play electric guitar in a trio with bass and drums. Boogie, shuffle, and slow blues rhythms, licks, double stops, chords, and bass patterns are presented for full and exciting blues. A CD with the music examples performed by a smokin' power trio is included for play-along instruction and jamming.
00695028 Book/CD Pack $19.99

100 Blues Lessons
Guitar Lesson Goldmine
by John Heussenstamm and Chad Johnson

A huge variety of blues guitar styles and techniques are covered, including: turnarounds, hammer-ons and pull-offs, slides, the blues scale, 12-bar blues, double stops, muting techniques, hybrid picking, fingerstyle blues, and much more!
00696452 Book/2-CD Pack $24.99

Electric Slide Guitar
by David Hamburger

This book/audio method explores the basic fundamentals of slide guitar: from selecting a slide and proper setup of the guitar, to open and standard tuning. Plenty of music examples are presented showing sample licks as well as backup/rhythm slide work. Each section also examines techniques and solos in the style of the best slide guitarists, including Duane Allman, Dave Hole, Ry Cooder, Bonnie Raitt, Muddy Waters, Johnny Winter and Elmore James.
00695022 Book/CD Pack $19.95

101 Must-Know Blues Licks
A Quick, Easy Reference for All Guitarists
by Wolf Marshall

Now you can add authentic blues feel and flavor to your playing! Here are 101 definitive licks – plus a demonstration CD – from every major blues guitar style, neatly organized into easy-to-use categories. They're all here, including Delta blues, jump blues, country blues, Memphis blues, Texas blues, West Coast blues, Chicago blues, and British blues.
00695318 Book/CD Pack $17.95

Fretboard Roadmaps Blues Guitar
for Acoustic and Electric Guitar
by Fred Sokolow

These essential fretboard patterns are roadmaps that all great blues guitarists know and use. This book teaches how to: play lead and rhythm anywhere on the fretboard, in any key; play a variety of lead guitar styles; play chords and progressions anywhere on the fretboard, in any key; expand chord vocabulary; learn to think musically, the way the pros do.
00695350 Book/CD Pack $14.95

The Road to Robert Johnson
The Genesis and Evolution of Blues in the Delta from the Late 1800s Through 1938
by Edward Komara

This book traces the development of the legendary Robert Johnson's music in light of the people and songs that directly and indirectly influenced him. It includes much information about life in the Delta from the late 1800s to Johnson's controversial death in 1938, and features fascinating historical photos, maps, musical examples, and much more.
00695388 .... $14.95

12-Bar Blues
by Dave Rubin

The term "12-bar blues" has become synonymous with blues music and is the basis for an incredible body of jazz, rock 'n' roll, and other forms of popular music. This book/CD pack is solely devoted to providing guitarists with all the technical tools necessary for playing 12-bar blues with authority. The CD includes 24 full-band tracks. Covers: boogie, shuffle, swing, riff, and jazzy blues progressions; Chicago, minor, slow, bebop, and other blues styles; soloing, intros, turnarounds, and more.
00695187 Book/CD Pack $18.99

Smokin' Blues Guitar
by Smokin' Joe Kubek with Dave Rubin

Texas blues guitar legend Smokin' Joe Kubek and acclaimed author and music historian Dave Rubin have teamed up to create this one-of-a-kind DVD/book bundle, featuring a high-definition DVD with Smokin' Joe himself demonstrating loads of electric blues licks, riffs, concepts, and techniques straight from his extensive arsenal. The companion book, co-written with Dave Rubin, provides standard notation and tablature for every smokin' example on the DVD, as well as bonus instructional material, and much more!
00696469 Book/DVD Pack $24.99

Blues You Can Use Chord Book
by John Ganapes

A reference guide to blues, R&B, jazz, and rock rhythm guitar, with hundreds of voicings, chord theory construction, chord progressions and exercises and much more. The Blues You Can Use Book Of Guitar Chords is useful for the beginner to advanced player.
00695082 .... $14.95

More Blues You Can Use
by John Ganapes

A complete guide to learning blues guitar, covering scales, rhythms, chords, patterns, rakes, techniques, and more. CD includes 13 full-demo solos.
00695165 Book/CD Pack $19.95

Blues Licks You Can Use
by John Ganapes

Contains music and performance notes for 75 hot lead phrases, covering styles including up-tempo and slow blues, jazz-blues, shuffle blues, swing blues and more! CD features full-band examples.
00695386 Book/CD Pack $16.95

HAL•LEONARD® CORPORATION

7777 W. BLUEMOUND RD. P.O. BOX 13819 MILWAUKEE, WI 53213

www.halleonard.com

Prices, availability, and contents subject to change without notice. Some products may not be available outside the U.S.A.

0516

HAL•LEONARD® GUITAR PLAY-ALONG

AUDIO ACCESS INCLUDED

This series will help you play your favorite songs quickly and easily. Just follow the tab and listen to the audio to the hear how the guitar should sound, and then play along using the separate backing tracks. Audio files also include software to slow down the tempo without changing pitch. The melody and lyrics are included in the book so that you can sing or simply follow along.

INCLUDES TAB

VOL. 1 – ROCK	00699570 / $16.99
VOL. 2 – ACOUSTIC	00699569 / $16.99
VOL. 3 – HARD ROCK	00699573 / $17.99
VOL. 4 – POP/ROCK	00699571 / $16.99
VOL. 6 – '90S ROCK	00699572 / $16.99
VOL. 7 – BLUES	00699575 / $17.99
VOL. 8 – ROCK	00699585 / $16.99
VOL. 9 – EASY ACOUSTIC SONGS	00151708 / $16.99
VOL. 10 – ACOUSTIC	00699586 / $16.95
VOL. 11 – EARLY ROCK	00699579 / $14.95
VOL. 12 – POP/ROCK	00699587 / $14.95
VOL. 13 – FOLK ROCK	00699581 / $15.99
VOL. 14 – BLUES ROCK	00699582 / $16.99
VOL. 15 – R&B	00699583 / $16.99
VOL. 16 – JAZZ	00699584 / $15.95
VOL. 17 – COUNTRY	00699588 / $16.99
VOL. 18 – ACOUSTIC ROCK	00699577 / $15.95
VOL. 19 – SOUL	00699578 / $15.99
VOL. 20 – ROCKABILLY	00699580 / $14.95
VOL. 21 – SANTANA	00174525 / $17.99
VOL. 22 – CHRISTMAS	00699600 / $15.99
VOL. 23 – SURF	00699635 / $15.99
VOL. 24 – ERIC CLAPTON	00699649 / $17.99
VOL. 25 – THE BEATLES	00198265 / $17.99
VOL. 26 – ELVIS PRESLEY	00699643 / $16.99
VOL. 27 – DAVID LEE ROTH	00699645 / $16.95
VOL. 28 – GREG KOCH	00699646 / $16.99
VOL. 29 – BOB SEGER	00699647 / $15.99
VOL. 30 – KISS	00699644 / $16.99
VOL. 31 – CHRISTMAS HITS	00699652 / $14.95
VOL. 32 – THE OFFSPRING	00699653 / $14.95
VOL. 33 – ACOUSTIC CLASSICS	00699656 / $17.99
VOL. 34 – CLASSIC ROCK	00699658 / $17.99
VOL. 35 – HAIR METAL	00699660 / $17.99
VOL. 36 – SOUTHERN ROCK	00699661 / $16.95
VOL. 37 – ACOUSTIC UNPLUGGED	00699662 / $22.99
VOL. 38 – BLUES	00699663 / $16.95
VOL. 39 – '80S METAL	00699664 / $16.99
VOL. 40 – INCUBUS	00699668 / $17.95
VOL. 41 – ERIC CLAPTON	00699669 / $17.99
VOL. 42 – COVER BAND HITS	00211597 / $16.99
VOL. 43 – LYNYRD SKYNYRD	00699681 / $17.95
VOL. 44 – JAZZ	00699689 / $16.99
VOL. 45 – TV THEMES	00699718 / $14.95
VOL. 46 – MAINSTREAM ROCK	00699722 / $16.95
VOL. 47 – HENDRIX SMASH HITS	00699723 / $19.99
VOL. 48 – AEROSMITH CLASSICS	00699724 / $17.99
VOL. 49 – STEVIE RAY VAUGHAN	00699725 / $17.99
VOL. 50 – VAN HALEN 1978-1984	00110269 / $17.99
VOL. 51 – ALTERNATIVE '90S	00699727 / $14.99
VOL. 52 – FUNK	00699728 / $15.99
VOL. 53 – DISCO	00699729 / $14.99
VOL. 54 – HEAVY METAL	00699730 / $15.99
VOL. 55 – POP METAL	00699731 / $14.95
VOL. 56 – FOO FIGHTERS	00699749 / $15.99
VOL. 59 – CHET ATKINS	00702347 / $16.99
VOL. 62 – CHRISTMAS CAROLS	00699798 / $12.95
VOL. 63 – CREEDENCE CLEARWATER REVIVAL	00699802 / $16.99
VOL. 64 – THE ULTIMATE OZZY OSBOURNE	00699803 / $17.99
VOL. 66 – THE ROLLING STONES	00699807 / $17.99
VOL. 67 – BLACK SABBATH	00699808 / $16.99

VOL. 68 – PINK FLOYD – DARK SIDE OF THE MOON	00699809 / $16.99
VOL. 69 – ACOUSTIC FAVORITES	00699810 / $16.99
VOL. 70 – OZZY OSBOURNE	00699805 / $16.99
VOL. 71 – CHRISTIAN ROCK	00699824 / $14.95
VOL. 73 – BLUESY ROCK	00699829 / $16.99
VOL. 74 – SIMPLE STRUMMING SONGS	00151706 / $19.99
VOL. 75 – TOM PETTY	00699882 / $16.99
VOL. 76 – COUNTRY HITS	00699884 / $14.95
VOL. 77 – BLUEGRASS	00699910 / $15.99
VOL. 78 – NIRVANA	00700132 / $16.99
VOL. 79 – NEIL YOUNG	00700133 / $24.99
VOL. 80 – ACOUSTIC ANTHOLOGY	00700175 / $19.95
VOL. 81 – ROCK ANTHOLOGY	00700176 / $22.99
VOL. 82 – EASY SONGS	00700177 / $14.99
VOL. 83 – THREE CHORD SONGS	00700178 / $16.99
VOL. 84 – STEELY DAN	00700200 / $16.99
VOL. 85 – THE POLICE	00700269 / $16.99
VOL. 86 – BOSTON	00700465 / $16.99
VOL. 87 – ACOUSTIC WOMEN	00700763 / $14.99
VOL. 89 – REGGAE	00700468 / $15.99
VOL. 90 – CLASSICAL POP	00700469 / $14.99
VOL. 91 – BLUES INSTRUMENTALS	00700505 / $15.99
VOL. 92 – EARLY ROCK INSTRUMENTALS	00700506 / $15.99
VOL. 93 – ROCK INSTRUMENTALS	00700507 / $16.99
VOL. 94 – SLOW BLUES	00700508 / $16.99
VOL. 95 – BLUES CLASSICS	00700509 / $14.99
VOL. 99 – ZZ TOP	00700762 / $16.99
VOL. 100 – B.B. KING	00700466 / $16.99
VOL. 101 – SONGS FOR BEGINNERS	00701917 / $14.99
VOL. 102 – CLASSIC PUNK	00700769 / $14.99
VOL. 103 – SWITCHFOOT	00700773 / $16.99
VOL. 104 – DUANE ALLMAN	00700846 / $16.99
VOL. 105 – LATIN	00700939 / $16.99
VOL. 106 – WEEZER	00700958 / $14.99
VOL. 107 – CREAM	00701069 / $16.99
VOL. 108 – THE WHO	00701053 / $16.99
VOL. 109 – STEVE MILLER	00701054 / $16.99
VOL. 110 – SLIDE GUITAR HITS	00701055 / $16.99
VOL. 111 – JOHN MELLENCAMP	00701056 / $14.99
VOL. 112 – QUEEN	00701052 / $16.99
VOL. 113 – JIM CROCE	00701058 / $15.99
VOL. 114 – BON JOVI	00701060 / $16.99
VOL. 115 – JOHNNY CASH	00701070 / $16.99
VOL. 116 – THE VENTURES	00701124 / $16.99
VOL. 117 – BRAD PAISLEY	00701224 / $16.99
VOL. 118 – ERIC JOHNSON	00701353 / $16.99
VOL. 119 – AC/DC CLASSICS	00701356 / $17.99
VOL. 120 – PROGRESSIVE ROCK	00701457 / $14.99
VOL. 121 – U2	00701508 / $16.99
VOL. 122 – CROSBY, STILLS & NASH	00701610 / $16.99
VOL. 123 – LENNON & MCCARTNEY ACOUSTIC	00701614 / $16.99
VOL. 125 – JEFF BECK	00701687 / $16.99
VOL. 126 – BOB MARLEY	00701701 / $16.99
VOL. 127 – 1970S ROCK	00701739 / $16.99
VOL. 128 – 1960S ROCK	00701740 / $14.99
VOL. 129 – MEGADETH	00701741 / $16.99
VOL. 130 – IRON MAIDEN	00701742 / $17.99
VOL. 131 – 1990S ROCK	00701743 / $14.99
VOL. 132 – COUNTRY ROCK	00701757 / $15.99
VOL. 133 – TAYLOR SWIFT	00701894 / $16.99
VOL. 134 – AVENGED SEVENFOLD	00701906 / $16.99
VOL. 135 – MINOR BLUES	00151350 / $17.99

VOL. 136 – GUITAR THEMES	00701922 / $14.99
VOL. 137 – IRISH TUNES	00701966 / $15.99
VOL. 138 – BLUEGRASS CLASSICS	00701967 / $14.99
VOL. 139 – GARY MOORE	00702370 / $16.99
VOL. 140 – MORE STEVIE RAY VAUGHAN	00702396 / $17.99
VOL. 141 – ACOUSTIC HITS	00702401 / $16.99
VOL. 143 – SLASH	00702425 / $19.99
VOL. 144 – DJANGO REINHARDT	00702531 / $16.99
VOL. 145 – DEF LEPPARD	00702532 / $17.99
VOL. 146 – ROBERT JOHNSON	00702533 / $16.99
VOL. 147 – SIMON & GARFUNKEL	14041591 / $16.99
VOL. 148 – BOB DYLAN	14041592 / $16.99
VOL. 149 – AC/DC HITS	14041593 / $17.99
VOL. 150 – ZAKK WYLDE	02501717 / $16.99
VOL. 151 – J.S. BACH	02501730 / $16.99
VOL. 152 – JOE BONAMASSA	02501751 / $19.99
VOL. 153 – RED HOT CHILI PEPPERS	00702990 / $19.99
VOL. 155 – ERIC CLAPTON – FROM THE ALBUM UNPLUGGED	00703085 / $16.99
VOL. 156 – SLAYER	00703770 / $17.99
VOL. 157 – FLEETWOOD MAC	00101382 / $16.99
VOL. 158 – ULTIMATE CHRISTMAS	00101889 / $14.99
VOL. 159 – WES MONTGOMERY	00102593 / $19.99
VOL. 160 – T-BONE WALKER	00102641 / $16.99
VOL. 161 – THE EAGLES – ACOUSTIC	00102659 / $17.99
VOL. 162 – THE EAGLES HITS	00102667 / $17.99
VOL. 163 – PANTERA	00103036 / $17.99
VOL. 164 – VAN HALEN 1986-1995	00110270 / $17.99
VOL. 165 – GREEN DAY	00210343 / $17.99
VOL. 166 – MODERN BLUES	00700764 / $16.99
VOL. 167 – DREAM THEATER	00111938 / $24.99
VOL. 168 – KISS	00113421 / $16.99
VOL. 169 – TAYLOR SWIFT	00115982 / $16.99
VOL. 170 – THREE DAYS GRACE	00117337 / $16.99
VOL. 171 – JAMES BROWN	00117420 / $16.99
VOL. 172 – THE DOOBIE BROTHERS	00119670 / $16.99
VOL. 174 – SCORPIONS	00122119 / $16.99
VOL. 175 – MICHAEL SCHENKER	00122127 / $16.99
VOL. 176 – BLUES BREAKERS WITH JOHN MAYALL & ERIC CLAPTON	00122132 / $19.99
VOL. 177 – ALBERT KING	00123271 / $16.99
VOL. 178 – JASON MRAZ	00124165 / $17.99
VOL. 179 – RAMONES	00127073 / $16.99
VOL. 180 – BRUNO MARS	00129706 / $16.99
VOL. 181 – JACK JOHNSON	00129854 / $16.99
VOL. 182 – SOUNDGARDEN	00138161 / $17.99
VOL. 183 – BUDDY GUY	00138240 / $17.99
VOL. 184 – KENNY WAYNE SHEPHERD	00138258 / $17.99
VOL. 185 – JOE SATRIANI	00139457 / $17.99
VOL. 186 – GRATEFUL DEAD	00139459 / $17.99
VOL. 187 – JOHN DENVER	00140839 / $17.99
VOL. 188 – MÖTLEY CRUE	00141145 / $17.99
VOL. 189 – JOHN MAYER	00144350 / $17.99
VOL. 191 – PINK FLOYD CLASSICS	00146164 / $17.99
VOL. 192 – JUDAS PRIEST	00151352 / $17.99

Prices, contents, and availability subject to change without notice.

Complete song lists available online.

HAL•LEONARD®
www.halleonard.com

0817